MEANING IN HISTORY

MEANING IN HISTORY

W. DILTHEY'S THOUGHTS
ON HISTORY AND SOCIETY

EDITED AND INTRODUCED BY

H. P. RICKMAN

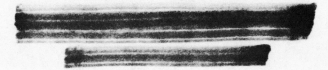

London
GEORGE ALLEN & UNWIN LTD
RUSKIN HOUSE MUSEUM STREET

Printed in Great Britain
in 10 on 11pt. Pilgrim type
by East Midland Printing Company Limited
Bury St. Edmunds, Suffolk

ACKNOWLEDGEMENTS

The texts, pages 66 to 168 are taken from Volume VII of Dilthey's works, published by the Teubner Verlag, Stuttgart. The translation was made with the permission, which I gratefully acknowledge, of B. G. Teubner, Verlagsgesellschaft mbH, Stuttgart.

CONTENTS

Contents

GENERAL INTRODUCTION

Dilthey's thought is very much alive today. In the spheres of history, biography and sociology one frequently comes upon ideas which have their—sometimes unacknowledged—source in his work. In other cases brief references to his importance are coupled with a recognition of the difficulties of presenting his ideas. For instance Mr F. Stern (in his selection of texts about history 'The Varieties of History' 1957) pays tribute to Dilthey's continuing influence. 'It is only in the last decade or so that the implications of Dilthey's historical thought have been elaborated and, to some extent, popularized.' Yet he has to say that some of the greatest historians 'Burkhardt, Croce, Dilthey and Pieter Geyl for example—had to be omitted because none of their shorter writings embodied the essence of their thought sufficiently to be truly representative. Similarly Professor Hughes (in Consciousness and Society 1959) speaks of Dilthey's 'enormous influence' and claims that 'the present study itself, in conception and orientation, has its origins in the canons for the philosophical investigation of society which Dilthey originally established'. He must acknowledge too 'In a study like this it is obviously impossible to present any complete analysis of the work of so versatile and complex a thinker as Dilthey.'

One could certainly continue this list of testimonies to Dilthey's importance. His sense of the value of individuals and his insight into the wealth and variety of the historical scene can be a source of inspiration to all who are concerned with human affairs. For practising historians his extensive writings retain a special interest as they deal with many of the problems which touch their work, with philology and source criticism, with the use of biographical material, with the interpretation of cultural phenomena and political actions, with the analysis of institutions and organizations and with the relevance of systematic studies such as economics, psychology or comparative jurisprudence to the reconstruction of historical events. He also discussed—more generally—the nature of historical knowledge, the place of valuations in historical accounts and the way in which the historian can tell a meaningful story.

Dilthey not only deserves justice as one of the great originators of our modern ways of thinking but should also be heard as one who has still a fruitful contribution to make to the current discussions on the nature and methods of history. For this reason I have selected and arranged passages from his maturest writings on this subject to make as continuous a text as possible. To these I have added an introduction which provides a brief account of Dilthey's life and writings and a sketch of the broad outlines of his theory of history. Technical discussions on Dilthey's philosophic position—his theory of knowledge for instance—which might be of interest to professional philosophers have been avoided as they would have made the book less accessible to the more general reader.

I. THE IMPORTANCE OF HISTORY

The importance of history and the equal importance of reflecting on its nature, method and influence is obvious and needs little justification. History is one of the forms of disciplined research by means of which the human mind satisfies its curiosity and orientates itself in the world. Its subject matter is the human past and the way the present has come about. The historian, to promote the advance of his discipline, must—like other research workers—take stock of his subject periodically and reflect on the nature and methods of history. He must consider fresh developments of various kinds; the use of new types of evidence—of church registers, court proceedings or state archives—the extension of subject matter, for instance, from diplomatic to social history, and the switch of interest from rulers and warriors to peasants and workers. He has to reflect on the use of techniques made available by the advance of different sciences: chemical tests to establish the genuineness of documents, or statistical methods to pre-

sent economic trends. Finally, he must weigh the relevance
to his research of generalizations which the progress of
different disciplines such as psychology, economics, social
anthropology and sociology provide. Faced with problems
such as these the thoughtful historian is forced to step outside his daily routine to reconsider the nature of his subject
and to redefine the scale on which he works and the aims he
pursues.

But history is not a specialized subject of interest only to
historians. It concerns us all. We look to it for an understanding of the world we live in, for an illumination of human
nature unfolding its potentialities in the course of time and
even for some hints about the future which may guide our
actions. Indeed, throughout the ages human beings have felt
that they received from history a revelation of the workings
of destiny and its purposes with man. To the interpretation of
this revelation they have brought their own points of view.
Confident and optimistic spirits to whom, on the whole, life
seemed good, saw, in the course of history, the forward march
towards a splendid present and an even more splendid future.
Saddened and oppressed minds saw only a futile meandering,
or even a plunge towards disaster of which they tried to warn
their contemporaries. Religious thinkers saw in history, dimly
or clearly, the working of God's purpose, liberals the spread
of free institutions. Thus, in their views of history, individuals
or whole ages have expressed their own conceptions of life.
Because such conceptions govern not only what we select as
relevant from the mass of facts, but also what forces we
believe determine the course of events, they colour historical
presentation. This presentation, in turn, is adduced to justify
the original point of view. In short, our ideas of history reflect
our philosophic, religious, moral and political attitudes, and,
at the same time, reinforce them. Reflection on our idea of
history, in consequence, confronts us with our own presuppositions and can lead to understanding of ourselves and the
temper of our age. In this lies its importance for all of us and
for the historian it is, in addition, an aid to detachment. Every
age, therefore, which seeks to understand historical reality

and to become alive to its own deeper impulses must examine its attitude to history afresh.

2. DILTHEY: THE MAN AND HIS WORK

How historical understanding—untrammelled by metaphysical dogma and undimmed by prejudice—could be achieved and made to serve clear-eyed comprehension of his own troubled age and how, finally, this insight could free man for creative activity, was W. Dilthey's lifelong preoccupation. His hard-won conclusions have not, I believe, lost their relevance today.

The outer events of Wilhelm Dilthey's life were unspectacular and can be stated briefly. Born in the Rhineland in 1833, the son of a protestant clergyman, he was first destined for a theological career. His interest in history and philosophy turned him from this path. He became a philosopher though he retained his love for history throughout his life. In 1867 he was appointed Professor of Philosophy at Basel. From there he moved to Kiel and thereafter to Breslau. In 1882 he was called to Berlin where he remained till his death in 1911.

Greatly loved by his pupils and admired by his contemporaries he made a deep impression on the intellectual climate of his age. Many testimonies to the charm and greatness of his personality can be quoted. The poet, Hugo von Hofmannsthal, for instance, wrote of him in lyrical terms: 'Wonderful the atmosphere around this old man . . . spiritual shining autumnal air . . . the air of Athens, the most delicate, wise and unsentimental air there is . . .' '. . . winged conversation . . . wise cheerful, sparkling of ageless eyes . . . impassioned conversation, impassioned listening: joy, impatience, passion in both' '. . . this is what philosophizing means, this is what it means to live a philosopher's life' (Der Tag 1911) Professor Anna Tumarkin writing with the warm affection of a disciple tried to evaluate his significance for his age in an article published shortly after his death in 'Archiv für Philosophie' (1912) I quote a few lines: 'Our age having become conscious through historical studies of the relativity of every individual historical formation, needs an orientation which leaves unconfined the manifold of individual forms and the wealth of life which, in its totality, remains for ever incommensurable. This is the deep tendency which today, dominates all metaphysical research, all religious longing, all fluctuations of artistic feeling and all forms of the human studies.

'Nobody has more deeply experienced this fundamental tendency of our intellectual life in its generality or interpreted it more truly than Dilthey.'

Another pupil, Professor H. Nohl, wrote in his introduction to Volume IV of Dilthey's collected works: 'I have watched the growth of this book . . . and I shall never forget the struggle to the point of exhaustion of the mysterious old man who thought only of his task; nor shall I forget the passionate absorption in the historical world of the mind and all its potentialities which I was privileged to share with him. What Dilthey praised in Hegel—the objective immersion, in complete self forgetfulness, in the subject—was his own essential nature.'

Dilthey applied his passionate, and yet clear-sighted, interest, his capacity for hard work and the power to absorb himself in his material—all the qualities to which his friends testify—to a wide range of subjects. Firstly and above all, he was, of course, a philosopher and all his different preoccupations found their place in the development of a comprehensive philosophic point of view. This point of view he himself described as a philosophy of life because it expressed the conviction that philosophizing must be based on and concerned with the fullness of human life in its social and historical manifestations. He reacted thus against the aridity of philosophies which start from a thinking subject in whose veins no real blood flows and against the narrowness of a positivism which, in deference to the methods of the physical sciences, confines its range to what can be seen and touched. His philosophy, because of its flexible and undogmatic character, can hardly be called a system; yet he brought a distinctive approach to the different traditional spheres of philosophy; the theory of knowledge, moral philosophy, aesthetics and the philosophy of history. In every case he developed his theories—in accordance with his programme of a philosophy of life—in close relation to concrete manifestations of human life and the disciplines concerned with them. Thus he wrote perceptively on music which he loved, produced searching studies of great poets, discussed educational practice and theory at some length and shrewdly criticized the psychology of his day.

His preoccupation with history deserves special consideration. It followed from his conception of the place and importance of historical knowledge that, in addition to pursuing historical research for its own sake, he approached the understanding of almost any problem, any idea, any cultural manifestation, in terms of its historical development and its place in a historical context. Thus, about two thirds of the First Volume of his collected works—his 'Introduction to the Human Studies'— is occupied with a historical account of the growth of metaphysical thinking from the ancient Greeks onwards and the way in which the human studies are related to this development. Volume II contains an analysis of conceptions of man in the Fifteenth, Sixteenth and Seventeenth centuries in which the ideas of thinkers ranging from Melanchton, Zwingli and Calvin to Giordano Bruno, Spinoza and Hobbes are presented. Volume III is dedicated to studies on the History of the German spirit and deals with Leibniz and his age, with Frederick the Great and the German Enlightenment and with the growth of the historical spirit in the Eighteenth century. Volume IV contains an account of the young Hegel and sketches of the life and work of various German Idealists. In Volume VI aesthetic theories of the Seventeenth, Eighteenth and Nineteenth century are discussed. Volume VIII deals historically with the development of philosophies and world views. Volume IX contains a history of educational ideas from the time of ancient Greece to the Seventeenth century. In Volume XII contributions to the history of Prussia are collected (accounts of Stein, Humbold, Gneisenau, etc., as well as discussions on law reform, the development of the welfare state and the place of the monarchy).

All this historical work, ranging over most of the European

past—whether history pure and simple or history subserving the systematic grasp of some problem—is confined to the history of ideas. In this sphere he was an original researcher, using archives and unpublished material and showing great skill in interpreting it.

Thus, his reflections on history sprang from deep personal interest in and first hand knowledge of historical research. I emphasize this point for the historian is justifiably suspicious of a philosopher who has only a nodding acquaintance with history and wants to teach him his job.

The range and originality of Dilthey's work provided inspiration in many other spheres beside that of history. He made important contributions to literary criticism and suggested new lines for the development of psychology. To discuss these lies outside the scope of this book but a word on the relevance of his thought to the development of sociology may be in place.

To Dilthey sociology meant the kind of work associated with the name of A. Comte and he had no very high opinion of it. He considered specific work in the spheres of economics, comparative religion or comparative jurisprudence much more important. But, if we understand by sociology the systematic study of regularities within society, we can say that Dilthey was almost constantly occupied with it. In that sense sociology is the sister discipline of history. Both deal with the life of humanity, the former attempting generalizations about uniformities, the latter setting out the sequence of unique events. Hence Dilthey developed his methodology of the social sciences side by side with his theories on history. His analysis of understanding, classification of expressions, account of the objectifications of life and description of cultural systems, which are represented in the texts and discussed in the introductions, are all contributions to this methodology.

I will refer briefly to some salient points and students of sociology will be able to recognise their relevance to the subsequent development of the subject.

Firstly, the use of understanding provides the human studies with a method distinct from those of the physical sciences and thus frees them from subservience to the latter. As understanding is not a matter of penetrating intuitively into the minds of others but of realizing what their expressions mean, we are led on to an analysis of the range of expressions and of the way in which we understand them. Words, gestures and actions—which are also expressions because they reveal the agents' intentions—must each be understood in a different way; they provide the sociologist with different kinds of evidence.

Secondly, the understanding of expressions is based on familiarity with the social and cultural context in which they occur. This context of institutions, traditions, rules and conventions which modern social anthropologists call the 'culture pattern' and which Dilthey called 'the objective mind' or the 'objectifications of life' can and must become the subject of sociological research.

Thirdly, the study of these culture patterns can be made more effective if we distinguish various functional systems such as education or economic production. These systems can be understood in terms of the way they are organized to satisfy the human needs from which they arise.

There has certainly been some acknowledgement of Dilthey's importance in this sphere. For instance, Professor Talcot Parsons (in *The Structure of Social Action*) recognizes that the concept of understanding 'owes more perhaps to Dilthey than to anyone else'. Yet the extent of the debt which such great originators of modern sociology as Max Weber owe to Dilthey has been insufficiently recognized. Historians of the development of sociology frequently complain about the difficulty, obscurity and ambiguity of the concept of 'understanding' when a close study of Dilthey would have done much to mimimize these difficulties.

Perhaps it is also worth while to mention the decisive influence which Dilthey's work exercised on the development of the philosophic movement usually called 'existentialism'. Heidegger, considered one of the founders of this movement and probably Germany's most influential modern philosopher, has himself testified to this influence. In *Sein und Zeit* (p. 366) he wrote, 'Fundamentally the following analysis of temporality and historicity is solely concerned with preparing the way for the assimilation of the researches of W. Dilthey which the present generation has yet to achieve'.

Nevertheless, a number of factors combined to delay full recognition of Dilthey's importance. To start with, the sheer bulk of his works is rather forbidding. His collected works comprise twelve large volumes and several other books are not included in that collection. Secondly, his very virtues involved him in serious flaws of composition. Because of the range of his interests most of his works are fragments. His recoil from any form of dogmatism made him avoid any neat rounding off of theories. His sense of the complexity of problems and his great flexibility of mind drove him into ever new attempts to tackle problems from a new angle. Up to the end of his life this candid and subtle thinker continued to rearrange and rewrite his material. In his old age he faced, somewhat unhappily, a growing mountain of manuscripts, some of them dictated to students and never revised, and the final crowning of his life's work by a systematic presentation of a critique of historical reason eluded him.

Only when scattered reflections and the work of his last years were edited and published posthumously by his disciples and when some of them, above all Professor Misch (in his important introduction to Volume V and in his massive work *Lebensphilosophie und Phänomenologie* 1931) pointed out and developed some of their implications, did the full importance of Dilthey as an original philosopher emerge. By then his thought was beginning to be overshadowed by the meteoric rise of the more incisive and more melodramatic formulations of Existentialism. Now that the signs are multiplying that this philosophy is past the peak of its popularity German thinkers are returning to Dilthey's more balanced and less desperate view. At this very moment his collected works, long out of print—are being completed and gradually reprinted.

Dilthey never really made his mark on the English speaking world in spite of the fact that his cast of mind, his liberalism, his empiricism, his suspicion of metaphysics and his own sympathizing with the British empirical tradition as represented, for instance, by J. S. Mill, should make him congenial to Anglo-Saxon readers. The great obstacle was, no doubt, his style and the difficulty of translating it into English. Though he could write pithily and eloquently at times he is more often weighty and involved. The traditional German style of writing philosophy combined with his temperament to produce this result. From the former stems, no doubt, the constant preference for abstract rather than concrete expression, from the latter the tendency to express his sense of the complexity and inter-relatedness of things in the very structure of his sentences. In consequence, his main works have never been translated into English and all that is available to English readers is less than fifty pages of selected passages translated by Professor Hodges and included in his *Wilhelm Dilthey, an Introduction*.

Yet the very nature of his writing makes it impossible to represent his view adequately in brief quotations or by selecting some essays or articles summarizing his theoretical position. He has to be read in bulk and from that reading grows an appreciation of his subtle and elastic approach. Again and again he appears to repeat himself, to restate a previously drawn conclusion, but a closer reading shows a subtle change of emphasis, the introduction of a new aspect or some important qualification. This is why I have thought it so important to present a substantial part of one of his main works in translation.

Where Dilthey is mentioned at all in discussions or books on the philosophy of history it is usually as a kind of nineteenth century fossil, the fumbling forerunner of more recent thinkers and such labels as historicism are attached to his philosophy. Professor Hodges' two scholarly and penetrating books (the one already mentioned and 'The Philosophy of Wilhelm Dilthey') did not succeed in altering this climate of opinion radically. This was due, first of all, to there being no texts to which he could refer. Secondly, he dealt comprehensively with the whole of Dilthey's philosophic work, as well as with the influences which had shaped his thought, and did not attempt a detailed exposition of what he himself called Dilthey's chef d'oeuvre—namely the theory of history which is formulated in Volume VII. Finally, the philosophic climate

of Great Britain at the time—preferring precision to imaginative exploration, detailed research to broad vision and the
methods of the physical sciences rather than those of the
social studies—was not favourable to the appreciation of the
genius of this diffuse and tentative thinker.

Yet the very subject which occupied Dilthey above all
others throughout his working life—the nature of history and
the epistemological justification of its methods—has moved
into the forefront of public discussion in the last few years.
Many historians in this country, for instance, Barraclough,
Butterfield, Trevor Roper, Namier, Carr and Miss Wedgwood
have offered reflections on the nature and methods of history
and philosophers like I. Berlin and R. K. Popper have also
made notable contributions to these topics. Dilthey's thoughts
are particularly relevant to these discussions and it is the aim
of this introduction to relate them to this context.

3. THE SCOPE OF THIS WORK

Dilthey's final theories of history are assembled in the seventh
volume of his collected works. As well as two studies published earlier this volume contains fragments in different
stages of completion which had not been published before.
Some of these are manuscripts revised by the author; others
are unrevised dictations to students. This untidy body of work
contains some discussions of little interest today, extensive
accounts of the history of historiography, particularly in Germany and is, in places, repetitive. Yet this fragmentary and
sprawling work represents Dilthey's culminating achievement, his maturest reflections based on decades of concentrated reflection.

To make the main thoughts of this work accessible to English readers, I have made a drastic selection. Consideration of
the text itself and, where possible, the date of composition,
together with some pointers provided by G. Misch (in his
Introduction to the fifth volume) have encouraged me to
believe that Dilthey arrived at a new point of view in the
very last years of his life and so began to rewrite and rearrange his arguments. This point of view is characterized,

above all, by the emergence of the concept of meaning as the pivot of Dilthey's argument. My selection aims at showing Dilthey's final view and, wherever possible, I have used the last statement he made on any topic. In all I have selected and translated about a third of the text of Volume VII and arranged the sections so as to produce as readable, logical and continuous a text as possible. At the cost of occasional repetitions I have tried to preserve longish, unbroken sections of Dilthey's arguments. The occasional omission marks usually indicate the deletion of a few words or lines only. The chapter headings and the arrangement into chapters are my own and I have omitted Dilthey's own titles and sub headings which, obviously, could not reflect my arrangement of the text. The Introductions to the individual chapters are meant to underline the trend of the argument and to provide necessary explanations.

Perhaps I should also add a few words about the translation. One set of problems which faces the translator is concerned with the terms 'Geist', 'geistige Welt', 'objektiver Geist', and 'Geisteswissenschaften'. These terms convey quite clearly certain connections which underpin Dilthey's central arguments. The 'objektive Geist' is the creation of 'Geist' and constitutes the 'geistige Welt'. The latter is the subject matter of the 'Geisteswissenschaften' and in them 'Geist' grasps what 'Geist' has created. This connection cannot, as far as I can see, be fully conveyed in an English translation. 'Geist' I have translated as 'mind' and 'objektiver Geist' by which Dilthey refers to such things as language, poetry, religion, science, art, social organizations, as 'objective mind', but to translate the 'geistige Welt' as 'mental world' or as 'the world of the mind' would be misleading. By this term Dilthey means the world of thoughts, feelings and purposes embodied in physical manifestations. This sphere is distinct from those of mental processes and of physical things, yet based on both. To it belong such things as the English language, the play *Othello*, the game of chess and the Napoleonic code. All these are creations of individual minds but confront us with an objective existence of their own. To say that somebody's poetry is only in the world of the mind (if it means anything at all) means that he hasn't written it down; but the 'geistige Welt' contains poetry which has been written and can be found in books.

As the 'geistige Welt' arises from and is related to human life, one is tempted to call it the 'human world'. But this again is misleading. It includes too much—namely the physical and biological aspects of human life—and does not specify the relation to mental activity. That human beings differ in the colour of their skins is a fact about the human world; my footprints in the sand are part of that world; but neither skin pigmentation nor footprints are part of the 'geistige Welt'. Another tempting translation would be 'cultural world'. This would cover many aspects referred to by the German term and, indeed, if it were used in the wide sense employed by modern social anthropology, it would be adequate. But as 'cultural' is not commonly applied to legal works or scientific treatises it, too, would be misleading. When using this term Dilthey refers to the totality of what has been created, moulded, or affected by our minds, so I have chosen 'mind-affected' world as the nearest possible translation. As 'the studies of the mind-affected world' would have been clumsy I have translated 'Geisteswissenschaften' as 'the human studies' because other possible translations—the moral sciences, the humanities, the cultural studies, or the social sciences—do not include all that Dilthey meant by this term, namely history, economics, sociology, social anthropology, psychology, comparative religion, jurisprudence, political science, philology and literary criticism, but *not* human biology, physical anthropology or physiological psychology.

These decisions left me with the problem of how to translate 'geistig' when it occurred in other connections. Different solutions had to be found for different contexts. Sometimes 'mental', sometimes 'cultural' or 'mind-affected' seemed to be most appropriate. When used as a noun 'das Geistige' could usually be rendered, without violence to Dilthey's intention, as 'mental content'.

Another set of problems is connected with Dilthey's constant use of a number of terms which convey his over-riding sense of the connectedness and inter-relatedness of things.

Again and again he uses 'Beziehung'; 'Verhältnis' and 'Verwandschaft' and these terms can only be rendered by 'relation' or 'relationship'. His favourite word is 'Zusammenhang' and this I have had to translate variously according to the context as 'connections', 'connectedness', 'context' and 'system'. For the composite formation 'Wirkungzusammenhang' which also occurs frequently I have used 'system of interactions' consistently as this conveys its meaning most clearly.

The translation presented many other problems but none of these affects the general trend of the argument.

4. PATTERNS AND MEANING IN HISTORY

To aid the understanding of Dilthey's thought and to underline its topical relevance I have concentrated discussion in this introduction on a few central topics and compared his ideas with those of some modern writers on history.

We shall deal with the topic of meaning in history first because, for several reasons, it leads us directly to the core of the issue. Firstly, the concern with meaning is, I believe, the impulse behind the construction of any philosophy of history. Secondly, contemporary concern with semantics and linguistic analysis has placed the concept of meaning in the centre of discussion and, therefore, makes it an obvious point of departure. It should be mentioned, though, that Dilthey's approach to meaning is not a purely linguistic one and provides a contrast and, I believe, a corrective to the current approach Thirdly, and this is the most important reason, Dilthey, as his views developed, placed increasing emphasis on the notion of meaning. Though he never completed the final systematization of his philosophy, I believe that much that is confusing and puzzling in his writings becomes clearer if we organize his ideas firmly around his concept of meaning.

Let us start our discussion with the obviously and intentionally vague, but fairly uncontroversial point that the historian is concerned with telling a meaningful story. A story is meaningful, we may say, if some relevant connections between facts or events can be made intelligible. Thus a pure chronicle, a pure setting down of disconnected facts, does not constitute history. More is involved, even if we confine ourselves to finding out 'the truth of this or that, not about things in general' to use a phrase of G. N. Clark. Thus our first crucial question arises: what intelligible connections can we discover in, or attribute to, the course of historical events and what assumption or assumptions can justify this process?

In considering some of the answers which have been given to this question we must, first of all, refer briefly to the famous or infamous metaphysical theory of history associated with the name of Hegel. We must do so not because it is still widely believed but because it continues to provide the bogey of a philosophy of history for contemporary thinkers; from it many have recoiled virtually to the extent of embracing a theory of 'one damned thing after another'.

Hegel's philosophy represents the logical opposite to a theory which sees no order in history whatsoever; history, it claims, is comprehensible because, in spite of the presence of blind passions and suffering in individuals and groups, the sequence of events represents an intrinsically rational process, the unfolding of the absolute spirit.

Hegel was no mean historian and was by no means as blindly insensitive and stupidly dogmatic as he is sometimes painted. His ideas gave considerable inspiration to historical research. In fact we can distinguish the empty metaphysical shell from a heuristic principle—a principle, that is, which stimulates further research—which is by no means foolish. The metaphysical shell, the assumption of a pervading rational process, is unwarranted, not only because it distorts the facts but also because it makes painstaking research superfluous. It is, as Dilthey himself pointed out, the death of real history. Croce has made the same point, saying that 'it tolls the bell for the death of the history of historians'. One need not labour this point; it has been made again and again. In fact, when reading the impassioned arguments of Professor Berlin or Professor Popper, one is faintly surprised to find that the adversary with whom they are locked in mortal combat is the long dead ghost of Hegel. Yet a heuristic principle which lurks in Hegel's approach gives it what plausibility it has and underlies his own historical insight. It is this; the historian, like any other researcher, approaches the subject of his study, however irrational its elements, with the assumption that it will lend itself to rational explanation. For instance—the psychologist approaching a neurotic patient assumes, without believing the patient to be acting rationally, that his obsession can be rationally explained. This surely is the general assumption of psycho-analysis, which does not seem to be tainted with Hegelianism.

Dialectical Materialism followed in the footsteps of Hegel. While departing from the assumption that the historical process was rational in itself it assumed it to be rationally understandable because it represented an overall pattern governed by the predominance of certain powers. Again, it contained a useful heuristic principle, namely the injunction to look for the influence of economic factors. But, insofar as it goes beyond this, it must be condemned on the same grounds as the Hegelian system.

Less philosophically sophisticated than the above doctrines is the general belief in progress. It came to be widely held and inspired the work of many historians. Recent historical experiences, rather than theoretical considerations, have undermined this faith. But it has also been recognized that the assumption of progress rests on a belief in absolute values. If this collapses we are left with the empty platitude that the past has produced the present. Only in isolated spheres in which some activities are directed towards the achievement of a goal can we talk about progress towards that goal (progress in physical science, or administrative efficiency). Again, we need not labour the point as these theories have received an extensive trouncing.

The theory that the history of mankind consists of the successive or overlapping life cycles, from birth to decay, of independent civilizations, arose to replace the no longer acceptable ideas of progress. This theory, associated with the name of O. Spengler and, in our time, with that of Professor A. Toynbee, opened up interesting vistas, provided a useful corrective to single track conceptions of history and initiated stimulating comparisons between civilizations. While it is beyond the scope of this book to do justice to this theory—or to any of those I have listed before—it should be mentioned that it has come in for damaging criticism at the hands of modern historians and philosophers. Because such a theory involves the marshalling of a vast mass of material its details could be faulted by specialists. The selection of facts which is offered as evidence for the theory has also proved vulnerable. Different theories, it has been suggested, could, with equal plausibility, be developed from different selections of facts. The analogy to organic nature implied in the theory that civilizations grow, flourish and decay like flowers or animals has been considered misleading. (Does it not obscure some outstanding characteristics of human history?) Finally, there is the question of whether or not the theory can provide us with definite conclusions about the time span involved in the history of civilizations and the stages they pass through. If it cannot, its use as a historical tool is gravely limited. Should we have to decide if the childish behaviour of a person is due to immaturity or senility the objectively ascertainable age of the person will provide us with invaluable evidence. But can we establish the age of a civilization? and even if we can does any particular number of years constitute its youth or middle age?

There remains the theory, at least as old as the Bible, but also propounded in our own day, that history can be understood in terms of the unfolding of the divine plan.

Perhaps it is not superfluous to say that to criticize this belief is not to attack the Christian view of life. Every Christian is, I presume, committed to the belief that God rules the world and that history is the unfolding of the divine plan. But this must be distinguished from the conviction that we can understand the individual events of history in terms of that plan.

It does not matter for our purpose whether God's plan is promoted by his direct intervention or, as probably most Christians believe today, unfolds in the ascertainable uniformities of this world. In either case the question is, 'Can we know the mind of God?' But to believe that the mind of God and the divine plan is rationally transparent and, therefore, knowable is Hegelianism rather than Christianity. Christians believe that God moves in a mysterious way, that his will is, to some extent at least, inscrutable, that revelation appeals to faith rather than to reason and that it reveals the inner meaning of all events rather than the connection between particular ones. Indeed, distinguished Christian theologians have maintained that even the crucial event of the resurrection is not a historically demonstrable fact but a sign revealing its inner meaning only to the eyes of faith. Thus a person can be a pious Christian and yet feel unable to use his belief in divine providence when he seeks historical explanations. An illustration outside the historical field may make this clear. A man who loses a leg in a motoring accident may believe deeply and sincerely that it was a punishment from God and a trial to which he must submit. This will inform his personal attitude and subsequent behaviour. But when he explains his accident in court nothing of this will be relevant, only such facts as that the road was slippery or that he had had two glasses of brandy earlier on.

Thus, without raising any intrinsic religious issue, we can ask whether a conception of divine providence is relevant and illuminating in historical research. Professor Butterfield's *Christianity and History* is a recent example of the attempt to establish—though not without ambiguity—that this is the case. But what, in fact, his arguments demonstrate is the meaninglessness of religious categories for historical understanding.

First of all it becomes clear that the Christian categories of sin, judgement, and so on, which he professes to discover in the structure of history he has put there himself by calling certain human tendencies sin and their consequences judgement. Secondly, he is forced to empty the concept of 'judgement', which he frequently uses, of all meaning in the historical context. On the one hand he points to certain disasters and defeats in history and calls them judgement; on the other, to avoid the cynical doctrines of identifying worldly success and failure with divine approval and disapproval, he retreats from this position. Judgements are only valid as self judgements (and thus not relevant to history); they are long term affairs; all human things lie under judgement and, finally, what may appear to be a judgement may only be a trial. Surely if this means anything at all it means that the application of such terms as divine judgement to the explanation of historical events is not only unsafe and meaningless but presumptuous.

If we have grown sceptical of theories which attribute patterns and meaning in history to the unfolding of the absolute spirit, the movement of the juggernaut of economic necessity, the inevitable forward march of progress, the ordered life cycles of civilization or the guiding hand of God, are we left with an ocean of unconnected facts following each other without rhyme or reason? And how can the historian tell a meaningful story? The answer which some historians have given places the burden of importing patterns and meaning into the course of events on the historian himself. Professor Carr, for instance, wrote in 'The New Society' 'For me the pattern in history is what is put there by the historian. History is itself the pattern into which the historian weaves his material, without pattern there can be no history. Pattern can only be the product of mind—the mind of the historian working on the events of the past.' There can be no doubt of the elements of truth in this approach. Historiography *is* the selection, arranging and interpreting of historical material. But can this be the whole of the story? Is it not a counsel of despair to resign ourselves to complete subjectivity? Are there not after all *some* patterns to be discovered in the course of events and, even if patterns can only be the product of mind, need the mind be that of the historian? After all, human beings—the actors in history—organize and interpret their lives and thus produce patterns which the historian can recapture objectively.

This leads us to Dilthey's own decisive and illuminating contribution to the disentangling of this problem.

The propounders of these various solutions were all motivated ultimately by the sense of facing an arid alternative; either the historian is faced by an assembly of disconnected facts which he can only record as a chronicler—thus falling victim to pedantry and antiquarianism—or, if he is not content to produce purely subjective arrangements, he must embrace a metaphysical or religious theory of history which attributes a total meaning to it. This sense of being driven by fear of historical nihilism into the arms of metaphysics has been forcibly expressed by contemporary historians. Professor Butterfield, for instance, felt himself obliged to take up the position he did because of the need 'to fill the story with significance'. Professor Barraclough (in a broadcast, a review in the *Times Educational Supplement* and in an essay '*History in a Changing World*') repeatedly insisted on the need for an 'end outside history' and 'a new set of values' to protect us from pedantry and antiquarianism.

Dilthey rejected a metaphysics of history and a heaping up of disjointed and meaningless facts as the horns of an inescapable dilemma. Human life and history are meaningful. This is one of the cornerstones of his approach. There is, indeed, nothing like *the* meaning of life or of history and, if there were it would not concern the historian in his research. But, on the other hand, there is—in a quite unmysterious way—meaning everywhere in life and it is with this kind of meaning that the historian, too, is concerned.

It is a matter of empirical fact and not of metaphysical speculation that we experience life in terms of patterns, connections and relationships which constitute for us the meaning of our experiences and indeed of our lives. Let us give a trivial example of how a human being always finds himself in interpreted and meaningful situations. Take a man sitting by the window of his drawing-room. The scent of roses coming from the garden gives him a pleasure and thus means something to him. It also means something to him because of the effort he has put into buying and planting these roses over the years. The size of the window which lets in insufficient light has always irritated him and is, therefore, significant to him. One of these days he will do something about it. The day means something to him because it is his wife's birthday. As he thinks of her days of his life stand out as meaningful turning points; the day they first met or the day of their engagement and their wedding day. He sees his brother entering the room and from his pinched appearance concludes that he has a headache. He interprets it as the after effects of influenza. He watches him opening the sideboard and understands that he is looking for aspirins. That his brother has a headache also means something to him; it causes him anxiety and this anxiety prompts him to action, perhaps to calling the doctor.

In this example we can distinguish different ways in which our experience is organized. Firstly, we note structural relations between our mental acts. Thoughts, for instance, arouse feelings and feelings prompt resolutions. Secondly, we see ourselves in dynamic interaction with an environment which pleases or frustrates us and affects us, not only as detached observers, but as creatures who feel, evaluate, hope and strive. We, in turn, affect this environment in accordance with our plans and purposes. Thirdly, we perceive significant relationships within our experience. We recognize physical manifestations—pinched features and the opening of drawers as well as spoken or written words—as signs of mental states. We see things as parts of a whole or as means to an end. There are, of course, important differences between the different senses of 'meaning', between, for instance, 'what something means' and 'what something means to somebody'. These have to be analysed and discussed. But, together, they constitute the ways in which we experience the world as meaningful.

We have emphasized, to start with, the meaning things have for an individual and the way he appreciates meaning around him. But, of course, human beings are not just lonely Robinson Crusoes in the centre of worlds of their own. Human beings live in communities. On the basis of their capacity—already referred to—for interpreting physical manifestations as signs men establish communication and, hence, a sphere of common meaning; language, religion, conventions, art and law. They join in common actions and create institutions to serve common purposes. This organized and meaningful way of life is based on the individual's primary experience of meaning and, in turn, permeates and makes possible the meaning which his own experience has for him. Thus, from the life of an individual—indeed from any one of his experiences—to the life of mankind there stretches a world of meaning.

This human world permeated—in the sense described—with meaning is the subject matter of the human studies. In its temporal extension it is the subject of history. The special importance and unique position of history lies in the fact that this temporal extension is not an external and incidental feature superadded to the meaningful structure of life. All the meaning in human life is linked to its temporal structure. To a momentary consciousness unaware of past and future the world would not be meaningful at all. Such a pure consciousness, groping its way back to its own past and its place in the world by means of arguments, is, in fact, a misleading figment of the philosopher's imagination. Man's past, present and future interlock at every moment of his life and every experience is meaningful to him in terms of these temporal dimensions. It is understood in terms of the past, the cumulative effects of which he selectively remembers. I would not recognize a rose if I had not encountered it before. I might not appreciate it if I had not become accustomed to its scent and the quality of my appreciation would not be what it is, if I did not recall episodes of my life associated with roses. It is enjoyed or suffered at the moment and seen as helping or hindering plans or purposes projected into the future. These temporal structures of human life are essentially the same as those of the life of mankind in time with which history proper has to deal. For communities, too, experience their present in terms of the past, the recollection of which is preserved for them in tradition, and the future, in which collective purposes are to be realized. We may, therefore, say that human life, as such, has a historical character. This constitutes Dilthey's conception of the historicity of human life which exercised so great an influence on the development of existentialism. This conception is focal to Dilthey's whole theory of history. On the one hand it establishes the importance of history as the unearthing of the temporal structures of life for the understanding of its meaning. On the other it bases the methodology of history on the individual's understanding of what it is to be a human being in the world. Hence autobiography and biography provide the models for, as well as the steppingstones to, history proper.

These conceptions of Dilthey's form the basis of his answer to the question how the historian, without resort to metaphysical theories, can tell a meaningful story. Step by step Dilthey analysed the temporal and historical structure of human life and the way in which meaning arises in it, how this meaning is expressed and how it can be understood. He then proceeded to an account of how the meaning rooted in the awareness of individuals becomes embedded in the meaning of institutions, organizations and historical processes, what form it takes there, how it can be recaptured through historical evidence and lead to historical understanding. This, together with discussions of the nature of historical evidence and the processes for sifting it, constitutes his methodology of historiography presented in the passages translated in this book.

5. THE METHODS OF HISTORY AND SCIENTIFIC METHOD

The focal point of Dilthey's theory of history—and his most original contribution—is his conception of understanding and interpretation, through which meaning is recaptured. To avoid the one-sided and mistaken view of this understanding as a knack of intuitive insight, the notion of which he inherited from the Romantic movement, we must first envisage the wider framework of theory into which Dilthey placed his views on this subject.

The different views on the methods of history range from the conviction that history can—and must to be respectable—avail itself of the methods of the physical sciences, to the belief that—because of its subject matter, it has to use methods all its own. On this issue, too, Dilthey strove for a broadly based, intermediary, position which would do justice to what merit the extreme views contained.

History, like the physical sciences, is an empirical discipline and shares with them many methods of inquiry such as observation, classification and the framing and testing of hypotheses. Observation may, for instance, take the form of discovering and studying some old documents. These may be classified as records of business transactions and the hypothesis that a form of capitalistic enterprise flourished in a particular city at a particular date may be framed. This may suggest further lines of investigation by means of which the hypothesis can be tested. Again, the historian may use methods which are analogous to those of comparative anatomy. As the anatomist reconstructs an animal from a few bones, so can the historian reconstruct the life of a monastery from the ruins of a building, the tools and broken pottery found on the ground and perhaps a list of monies paid out by the monks during a certain period of time. Or the historian may throw light on an institution by placing it into an evolutionary series as the biologist does a species of animal. The historian may also use quantification and statistical methods to deal for example with economic changes or the rise and decline of classes.

There are, of course, differences in this sphere. Human affairs appear to be more complex, less easily analysable, less accessible to quantitative and precise presentation, than physical states of affairs. Experimentation is largely excluded by the nature of the subject; can only be used marginally for the testing of the genuineness and plausibility of evidence. (Is this document really 500 years old? Could heavily armed men really have marched from A to B in 10 days? These are the types of questions which can be settled experimentally.) But these differences are, on the whole, a matter of degree and do not raise questions of principle. Yet there appears to be a significant difference between history and science. The former deals with sequences of events, each of them unique, while the latter is concerned with the routine appearance of things and aims at generalizations and the establishment of regularities governed by laws. This, too, seems to be more a matter of emphasis and focus of interest than a fundamental distinction. In the course of his work the scientist must give an account of individual experiments and, sometimes, elaborate descriptions of sequences of individual events such as the origin of the solar system or the evolution of man, though his main concern is with the regularities involved in them. The historian, on the other hand, must deal with types of events which recur again and again; wars, revolutions, the founding of empires and struggles for power—though he must be concerned as much with their unique qualities as with the similarities between them. If, therefore, we distinguish sharply between historical method—the presentation of series of unique events—and scientific—the systematic grasp of regularities, we have to conclude that the actual disciplines of history and the sciences avail themselves, in different admixtures, of both methods.

We may say, then, that the historian is distinguished from the scientist because he is primarily concerned with individual sequences of events; but, to explain the connection between events, he must avail himself of regularities and refer to laws. What kind of laws are these? If the historian could, as Hegel and Marx believed, establish laws or trends in accordance with which the historical sequence of ever new and unique events took place, he would be discovering historical laws and would be producing something entirely unlike the generalizations of the scientist. But if the historian is to keep his feet firmly on the ground of experience he cannot do this. The laws which he can, and must, use are the laws of the different sciences and human disciplines. The findings of almost any science may be relevant; those of physics or chemistry to account for the superiority of certain weapons and, hence, for the outcome of a particular battle; those of botany to establish the rate of reafforestation in a particular country and, thus, to explain the limitations of its shipbuilding programme. The conclusions of the human studies, of economics, psychology or anthropology, as well as the broad generalizations established by experience and commonsense—such as 'power corrupts' or 'privileged classes cling to their privileges'—are, of course, of special relevance. Philology, concerned with the sifting of written sources, plays a special role as an auxiliary discipline. This point was recently made by Professor Trevor Roper in his inaugural lecture, '*History—Professional and Lay*'. He says 'although scientific laws are relevant to it and condition its course, these laws are the laws

of other sciences—of economics or geography or statistics—
they are not the laws of history.' But while history must avail
itself of the aid of different sciences it must not submit itself
to any of them—economics, military science or psychology
—as its master. The very attempt to make history scientific by
applying to it the laws of a science, the subject-matter of
which is assumed to be the dominant factor of history, stamps
history as dogmatic and unscientific. What factors—economic
conditions, military techniques, or theological beliefs—are of
decisive influence in any particular historical situation must
be decided empirically by studying the evidence.

Another point on which history is often considered to
depart from empiricism and, thereby, to distinguish itself from
science, concerns its use of concepts to represent its subject-
matter. In addition to dealing concretely with individual
persons—a Napoleon or a Hitler—and with individual events
such as the death of a king or the signing of a treaty, the
historian concerns himself with elusive entities such as
classes, nations and ages—even worse—with the religious spirit
of an age, the will of a nation or the interests of a state. This
may tempt him into viewing states, nations or ages as entities
possessing some form of metaphysical reality and endowed
with pseudo-personal qualities, like will, thought and intentions. It will draw him into a quagmire of false analogies. To
avoid this mistake he may recoil into reducing everything to
the actions of individuals. But this is an equally dangerous
and dogmatic narrowing of the field. Dilthey strongly condemned both extremes; he certainly believed that only individuals were empirically given entities, that only individuals
had feelings, thoughts and intentions. But he also believed
that, as a matter of empirical fact, individuals stood in certain
relationships to each other, were affected by common factors,
strove for communal goals and shared a common stock of
ideas and that these and similar facts were most conveniently
and most precisely referred to by assertions with such logical
constructions as nations, ages or classes as their subjects. Once
these concepts are considered as useful and perhaps necessary
logical constructions which refer to inter-personal factors there

remains little difference between them and some of the concepts of the sciences.

So far we have stressed that history, while distinct from the sciences in its emphasis on the individual, avails itself of intellectual processes which have their analogues in science, and, indeed, submits itself to the discipline of using the conclusions of science in some of its explanations. It may be worth while mentioning at this point that a modern discussion of historical method—Professor K. R. Popper's *The Poverty of Historicism*—follows, though, no doubt, unconsciously, this line of argument very closely. The fact that Dilthey can—in a sense to be explained later—be described as a historicist and that Professor Popper's essay is largely an attack on historicism must not blind us to the parallels. Popper defines historicism in an unusual way according to which Hegel and Marx, for instance, but not Dilthey can be classed as historicists, namely as 'an approach to the social sciences, which assumes that *historical prediction* is their principal aim and which assumes that this aim is attainable by discovering the "rhythms" or the "patterns" the "laws" or the "trends" that underlie the evolution of history.'

6. MEANING AND UNDERSTANDING

We must now turn to the outstanding difference between the physical sciences and history and, for that matter, all the human studies. This difference turns on the fact that history is concerned with human beings and the human world. We have already noted that the human world is permeated with meaning and that, in consequence, the relationships with which the historian is concerned are not merely causal relations—as is, crudely put, the case in the physical sciences—but meaningful relationships. The place of knowledge and explanation is, therefore, taken by understanding and interpretation.

Let me make the difference between causal and meaningful relations clearer by means of illustrations. Let us consider first the difference between the wind blowing down a tree and my felling a tree. In the first case all we can or want to know is the relation between the force of the wind as the cause and the splintering of the wood which is the consequence. In the second case there is, of course, a causal relation between the force with which the axe is wielded and the fall of the tree; but there is also quite a different relation which has to be taken into account if the situation is to become intelligible, namely that between my intention, the idea or purpose in my mind—and the action. In the case of the relation between wind or axe-stroke and the falling of the tree we have a sequence of events which we describe in terms of causality. In the case of relating my intention to the act I am directly aware of myself as a power exerting itself on the environment and the latter is therefore a meaningful relationship.

As a second illustration we might contrast a case of inter-action in the physical world, the wind and the tree, for in-stance, with a case of interaction between human beings. Somebody insults me and I slap his face. Ordinary causal relations are, of course, involved. Innervation of my muscles lifts my arm etc. Indeed, we might say that the insult is the cause of the assault. But this obviously does no justice to the situation. To be insulted I must understand the words and, perhaps, the way in which they are uttered. I must also appreciate the whole social situation. When I hit out my action stems from such things as my concern for my status, my sense of how insults should be dealt with in my society. In taking my revenge the actual infliction of pain may be a very minor consideration. I may be more concerned with the scorn I express, the humiliation I inflict—in other words, with the meaning of my action. It may be objected that I over-intellectualize what may be a spontaneous response, but I would maintain that men, even when they do not stop to reflect, act not in response to situations but in response to their ideas of situations which are coloured by a mass of traditions and conventions. These ideas determine the form of the assault, which might otherwise have taken many different forms. A slap in the face may appear appropriate while a kick on the shin may seem ridiculous and a knee thrust in the groin vulgar and brutal. In these cases, because

38

we are dealing with the actions of human beings, we have meaningful relations.

Understanding, the process of grasping meaning, is a mental operation which can be defined in terms of other mental operations as little as can seeing or reasoning. Dilthey's whole epistemology of historical insight hinges on the analysis of this process. Understanding, for him, is a technical term and will be used as such throughout this book though it represents a narrowing of the English usage. Understanding is insight into the working of a human mind, or, as Dilthey himself says, 'the rediscovery of the I in the Thou'. Thus I can understand why John paces up and down the room but not why my plant won't grow. In the latter case I would have to say, 'I know why it won't grow'. The notion of understanding would also apply to what human beings have produced; thus I might understand a poem as well as a gadget.

Understanding rests on what we might call an inside view of human nature which we all possess. We are certainly not all psychologically sophisticated; we have not analysed ourselves and traced out motives. Indeed, where we think that we know our motives we often delude ourselves; a spectator may understand them better. Thus we have no privileged psychological knowledge. Indeed, we are not talking about psychological knowledge at all but about something much more simple and fundamental. We know what it is like to be angry or happy, to remember or to make an effort towards a goal. We also experience certain connections in our mental life directly, how a memory may produce grief or desire and how such desire may prompt us to action. In addition, we experience the relation between anger and the clenching of our fists, between resolve and the commencement of action.

The employment of these basic insights allows us to understand other people. Such understanding is neither mysterious nor infallible. It can be described as based on a kind of analogical argument. This man is clenching his fists, I clench my fists when I am angry therefore . . . . Yet this already distorts the sense of *direct* insight we seem to have ('Surely I *see* that this man is angry?').

Here, then, lies the decisive difference between the natural

39

sciences and the human studies. The latter may never achieve the precision of the former but they have the incomparable advantage of moving in a world which, in a true sense, is familiar to us. The human mind can understand whatever it has created and the whole historical world spreads before us as a field of human activity, of the realization of human hopes and the suffering of misery and frustration by human beings. The natural scientist observes sequences of events and construes causal or other laws from them. In history we not only know that somebody saw the chance of a crown and acted to gain it, but also what it is to want something and to strive for it, which forms the inner link between these events. Not only the facts but also the connections between them lie open before us.

This understanding is not an obscure, unanalysable intuition, a mysterious flash of lightning, a gimmick which replaces disciplined intellectual work and makes it superfluous. It is a form of knowing which operates in the human sphere, avails itself of intellectual processes and interacts and co-operates with other intellectual processes. The examination of the way this understanding operates in historical research constitutes the methodology of that discipline.

Reflecting on our own lives we understand the meaning of life. We understand how experiences are coloured by past events retained in the memory, how successive periods of time represent the realization or frustration of aims, how we act on the environment and are influenced by it. When we pass from the understanding of our own lives to understanding those of others, when, that is, we turn from autobiography to biography we must still avail ourselves of the fact that the life under consideration had a meaning for the subject of the biography; that is, it was organized by a self and must be understood from that point of view.

Certainly, if we write biography, we bring our own point of view to bear on it; we select what seems important and interesting to us. This is inevitable and we cannot eliminate it. It brings in an element of subjectivity which we can control by our very awareness of it. But this is by no means all. We can produce a counterbalance to that subjectivity by understanding, that is, by grasping the point of view of the person under investigation. That person had himself decided what was important to him and interpreted his own life; these interpretations can guide us. This understanding is itself based on empirical enquiry. We gather letters, diaries and reports of the subject's conversations; we consider the actions which often speak eloquently of a man's intentions. If sufficient evidence is available we grasp, with some degree of object-ivity, the meaning which life had for the person we are describing, the inner organization or pattern of his life.

To put the point more explicitly; human life is not only meaningful; it is also articulate; it expresses its own meaning which we can understand. In this lies the difference between the studies of man and the natural sciences.

The life of an individual cannot, of course, be understood in isolation for it stands in a wider context. The individual par-ticipates in the life of the community and in different organ-izations; he is a child of his age. Thus a biography, having to take account of this fact, holds an uneasy balance between the history of a person and an account of a period, that is history proper. The contexts in which individuals stand can be understood—and here we have come to an important aspect of Dilthey's theory—in a way analogous to that in which we understand individuals because they consist of relations be-tween human beings and creations of the human mind. The actual context in which an individual stands is made up of traditions, beliefs, practices and a language which he shares with others and various organizations of which he is a member, such as a church, a branch of industry, a political party, a literary society. Because organizations such as these are designed to serve human purposes they can be under-stood. Let us take a chess club as a simple example. There is nothing mysterious, no metaphysical entity here. Human beings have founded it, use it and constitute it. Yet we can talk about the chess club and its history as distinct from talking about individuals. The club persists through changes of membership; its purposes are embodied in a constitution and in rules. It has a history and important events may be recorded in its minutes. It has property and a legal personality. Joining it affects the behaviour of individuals. The meaning of such an organization as a chess club, a university, a legal system, or even a state-organization, can become clear to the understanding in a way analogous to that in which we understand a person—once the relevant facts have been assembled. We see what purposes it serves, what values it realizes, what facts it considers relevant to itself. We understand all these individual systems, indeed, the whole of history, because everywhere we encounter what human beings have done, suffered and created. Everywhere pattern and meaning was experienced and created by those involved in the events and the historian's primary task is to recreate or to unearth these original interpretations.

In the case of the chess club—or a religion, a state, a legal system, we have before us what Dilthey calls an objectification of life, an example of objective mind which is part of the mind-affected world. Dilthey makes no metaphysical claims for the reality of these entities. They have their physical existence as marks on paper, bricks, and so on; their meaning is created and grasped by individual human beings. Yet it is methodologically important to retain them as logical units and not to attempt their psychological reduction. We really want to say such things as 'Poetry has influenced my life'. 'Protestantism is an important factor in the history of England'. In other words, we want to explain individual events and understand individual human beings in terms of the interpersonal contexts in which they stand and which have influenced them.

When we talk about the mind, objective mind, and the mind-affected world we must avoid the mistake of taking these terms in an intellectualistic sense. This, in fact, is the point at which Dilthey diverged emphatically from Hegel's use of these terms. The creations of the mind are expressions of the fullness of life; they exhibit the complexity of human nature and may reveal to the interpreter depths of which the creator himself was not really conscious. These depths of human nature become particularly accessible to interpretation in works of art or literature. Dilthey called this work of interpreting the products of human activity which reveal the qualities of human life, the hermeneutic art.

7. THE HISTORICAL IMAGINATION AND THE MATERIAL OF HISTORY

What Dilthey calls the understanding has figured in recent discussions as the historical imagination. Two broadcasts, M. Wight's 'What makes a good historian?' (*Listener* Feb. 17, 1955) and Professor Roper's 'Historical Imagination' (*Listener* Feb. 27, 1958) develop this concept in a way which is strikingly similar to that in which Dilthey presents understanding.

By the 'historical imagination' Mr Wight means 'the desire to enter the past, to understand it, to re-enact it'. He then refers to Michelet's assertion that 'the problem of historiography is the *resurrection* of life in its entirety' to Maintland's belief in the importance of grasping the thought of bygone ages and to Collingwood's theory that the historian's job is nothing but the re-enactment of past thought. Professor Trevor Roper defines historical imagination as 'the capacity to migrate into distant, foreign minds' and he asserts that its use means 'Making (the past) fully intelligible to us, by enabling us to enter, as it were, into the minds and passions of people who, in some way, seem very different from us' and this, he believes, is necessary if we are to get 'not merely accurate presentation but significant presentation'.

These quotations and—as far as I can judge from his writings, Professor Trevor Roper's whole approach to history —reflect Dilthey's views closely and bear witness to the continued importance of the theoretical framework which he developed. There are, of course, minor points of difference. Dilthey would, for instance, have criticized Collingwood's definition for singling out 'thought' and he would have quarrelled with Professor Trevor Roper's sharp distinction between the 'collecting, arranging, interpreting and publishing the evidence of history' and the use of the historical imagination.

As the concept of the 'historical imagination' may have a clearer and more precise meaning to the English reader than Dilthey's own term 'understanding' we may profitably adopt it in the further exposition of Dilthey's theory. We will then gain a clearer conception of the role of imagination in historical research. Can it form the basis of a disciplined approach? What role does it play in the gathering, selection and interpretation of historical evidence? This is the kind of question we shall have to discuss.

Imagination is obviously a general human capacity which individuals possess to varying degrees. It enters into innumerable activities such as the theory-making of the scientist, the creative work of the artist, the preparation of tasty meals, the understanding of other people and the writing of history. In each case the material it works on is different and, in the case of history, it is concerned with understanding human actions and their results. As well as being applied in different spheres imagination can be subjected to different degrees of discipline. In daydreaming or in the writing of romances it is more or less undisciplined; in scientific theory making and in historical research it can, and must, be disciplined by being linked to various intellectual processes and related to given material on which it is to work. In other words, the historian who claims that he has entered imaginatively into the mind of a historical figure or the spirit of an age and presents an imaginative reconstruction of the thoughts, purposes and feelings of a person or generation must also produce the evidence for his conclusions in terms of letters, speeches and contemporary accounts of the period. On this basis he claims the truth of his conclusions and can argue about them with his colleagues. To this rather than to a mere enumeration of facts, he would apply Ranke's programmatic statement about establishing 'what actually happened' (literally 'what it was really like').

The use of the imagination, Dilthey believed, entered into every operation of historical research and was, in turn, controlled by these operations. One of the operations involving imagination is interpretation. This must not be confused with the unravelling of the motives behind an action which may well be impossible and need not be part of the historian's task. Let us take an illustration. We know that at some point in history a chancellor of the exchequer, after some months in office, resigned. If we have such evidence as his budget proposals, the economic state of the country, the minutes of the cabinet, the letter of resignation and speeches of the people concerned, we may understand what happened. This understanding involves an imaginative reconstruction, on the basis of the evidence, of what was in the actors' minds. We grasp the chancellor's policy or economic and political intention, not only what he did but what he was trying to do. We comprehend the reasons why some things were done and others planned. These were in a human mind but they expressed themselves in actions and can, on that basis, be understood by the historical imagination. Motives are a different matter altogether. We may suspect that the chancellor was deeply imbued by patriotism or that he had the interests of a particular section of the community at heart, that he was devoured by ambition or oppressed by melancholy: or that, in his heart of hearts, he wanted to be rid of responsibility. All this we may never know (unless any of these motives become a purpose issuing into action) but need the historian be concerned with these matters? Dilthey did not think so. When he grasps the relations between intention, action and the ensuing actual consequence the historian understands the historical pattern of events. He does not need to ape the fictional omniscience of the historical novelist. He need not, therefore, apply the tenuous hypotheses of psychology nor trouble his intuitive faculties to probe the depth of the human mind. A theory of the historical imagination need not be a theory for making bricks without straw; it represents not a divinatory art but the disciplined use of a faculty. It is, surely, one aspect, at least, of the value of history that we know a man through what he does and not the other way round.

Next we may ask if the selection of relevant material apparently a much more down to earth task, also involves the exercise of the historical imagination. How do we really select what is historically relevant from the innumerable events which have occurred in the process of time?

There must obviously be some subjectivity in what the historian selects for his study. He will select in accordance with his interest, training and temperament and will, perhaps, also be influenced by the preoccupations of his age. This selection will refer to period and place (say sixteenth century Italy) to the scope of the investigation (the whole century or only part of it) and to the aspect to be studied (say economic life). This selection, even if practically always necessary, is, theoretically, of little significance. It usually represents the self-limitation of individuals who depend on others to deal with aspects of history which they leave out and does not involve a decision about the comparative importance of various factors in history.

The question remains; how do we select in terms of importance and relevance? Dilthey cuts through any rigid division between the scientific sifting and selecting of the evidence and the free play of the imagination by suggesting that the work of the historical imagination uncovers principles of selection for us. Understanding gives us insight into life; and selection, which decides importance, accompanies human life as it is lived. Wherever we encounter human life it is self-organized, has acquired patterns. What seems unimportant is forgotten. Landmarks decisive to the individual's development stand out in memory, are referred to and, perhaps, recorded. When we consider an individual, a group, or even an age, we find that, to a smaller or larger degree, it is centred around values and ideals which are held to be important. These ideals and values held subjectively by agents or groups of agents and grasped by the historian's imagination, provide at least one principle— though not the sole one—for the objective assessment of the relevance and importance of facts. To put this matter concretely; to ask how important economics or religion are in history is a metaphysical and probably nonsensical question. But, by exercising the historical imagination on the evidence available, we may be able to decide that religion played a decisive part in, for example, the life of St Augustine or in Europe in the thirteenth century. It then becomes important to understand the quality of the religion of this man or that age and to select and evaluate facts in terms of this central importance of religion. In one historical setting politics may provide the guiding thread; in another age economics may prove the central feature. In other words, again, the historian in his selecting and sorting of the facts, does not start from scratch. The historical course of events which he is trying to retrace, has already been experienced as meaningful by the actors involved in it. They have already selected and interpreted the facts and evaluated their own actions. These interpretations and evaluations are there for the historian not only in the historical accounts of eye witnesses, but in legal codes, business transactions, memoranda, sermons, poems and paintings. As the historian interprets these documents imaginatively he not only enters into the minds of strange people but also grasps patterns and connections between events as they presented themselves to the human beings involved in them.

Dilthey put this point by saying that we must understand a period of history as being centred upon itself and not just as a preliminary stage to our own time. It is, I think, essentially the same point which Professor Barraclough describes as 'the dogma . . . that the past exists for itself and that the historian's business is to reconstruct and recreate and relive it in loving detail' and he rightly calls it a historicist view. He is also right in considering the latter formulation not happily phrased. The past, of course, does not, in any ordinary sense of the word, exist at all. But the meaning of both formulations is clear enough. We cannot properly understand a past age by applying to it our own notions of politics or government, our own ideas and valuations. We can only understand it in terms of the institutions then prevalent, the ideas which animated the people who lived in it and the purposes which were then pursued.

In the interpretations which men of the past and, indeed, whole ages, have given to their lives and actions lies a firm starting point for the historian and, in grasping it, he can unify historical method. Of course, if matters are as Dilthey suggests, we cannot first establish the facts scientifically, collect, arrange and interpret them and afterwards exercise our historical imagination on them. There must, rather, be a pendulum movement between the processes. Having got hold of some facts we try to glean from them some imaginative insight; this will help us to arrange these facts and to discover the relevance of others. In the light of the new facts we can test, and perhaps modify, our original imaginative conclusions. Thus, gradually, we widen and deepen our inquiry through the interplay of these complementary methods. Historical imagination helps us to decide what the relevant historical facts are but the imaginative reconstruction is, in its turn, based on these facts.

There cannot be a logical, one-way construction starting with the simple and ending with the complex; Dilthey considered this to be an additional characteristic of the human studies which distinguishes them from the natural sciences; but it may well be that, in the light of modern research, things are somewhat similar in the physical sciences as well. I am not competent to decide on this issue.

The unearthing of the meaning events had for the actors involved in them, though a valid starting point, can, obviously, not be the whole of the story. If we ask about the meaning of an action, the meaning it had for the agent can only be a part, though an essential part, of the answer. This is so for two reasons in particular. First of all, the agent may not fully understand his own action or may even misinterpret it. Because of fundamental common features in human nature we may understand an action or expression though the author has remained unconscious of its meaning. We may know, for instance, from a person's behaviour that he is beginning to fall in love before he knows it himself. Secondly, the agent cannot know all the effects his actions will have; how, for instance, they will affect us. But we, considering the meaning of his actions, must take their consequences into account. To the assassin at Sarajevo his act was one of patriotic defiance. To those who organized his activity it was a move in a political game. To us the meaning of the action lies in its having started the chain reaction which led to the first world war.

Here we see an aspect of the meaning of events which provides us with an additional principle for selecting what is important. What has exercised greater or more lasting influence must figure more prominently; what has left little trace may remain marginal in historical accounts. As historical events continue to exercise an influence we may see them in new lights in successive ages. Hence, as Dilthey emphasizes, history has to be rewritten from time to time, though past histories may retain some abiding value and truth. A whole chain of events acquires new meaning as new links of it emerge. The football pool coupon filled in on Wednesday acquires a new meaning when it is found to have won a large sum on Saturday and new meaning again three months later when the winner has drunk himself to death. Miss C. V. Wedgwood discussing in a broadcast—*Listener*, Feb. 10, 1955 —the fact that history has to be rewritten in successive generations makes a point which is supplementary to Dilthey's theory. Because each generation, she asserts, brings a new point of view and new experiences to the consideration of the past, it finds different aspects more important and some periods more congenial than others. Dilthey's and Miss Wedgwood's theories on this subject obviously strengthen each other. Because, to take an example, we live in an age so largely dominated by scientific progress, we are apt to consider scientific developments in the seventeenth century as more important than the theological disputes of that time. But we also note and consider these early scientific researches important because we know now how influential the development which stemmed from them became for the subsequent centuries.

We can now see more clearly how understanding (or imagination) uncovers the meaning of an action, or sequence of actions and, thereby, provides us with criteria for selecting what is relevant and deciding what is important. Let me consider a simple schematic example which nevertheless represents the working of these principles in historical research. A does something which affects B and C and later, perhaps indirectly through C, me. I first get one aspect of the meaning of that action by imaginatively entering into A and understanding what his purpose was, how important it was to him and what meaning the action had for him generally. To understand whether, how and to what extent, his action affected B and C I have to enter imaginatively into their points of view. Obviously it was not just a chain of physical events which led from the murder of Ferdinand to the German ultimatum to France. How, finally, the action affects me, I understand in

D   49

the same way as I understand anything else which has meaning for me, namely, in terms of my own valuations, interests and aims, which are affected by this action.

Thus the extrapolation of the meaning of a historical event rests, according to Dilthey, on a threefold process: firstly, on the understanding of the point of view of the original actors; secondly, on the understanding of the meaning their actions had for those it directly affected; thirdly, on an assessment of these events in the light of the historian's own age, that is, in terms of their consequences in time and the ways in which they ultimately affected the historian and his age. Through the combination of these lines of approach we move towards fuller understanding, though we need not assume that 'the' meaning of an action can ever be fully exhausted.

8. HISTORICISM

The theory about the different points of view from which we must explore the meaning of a historical event guards the historian, on the one hand, from complete subjectivity, that is, from seeing things merely in the light of his own age or even his own preoccupations, but, on the other, from losing himself through antiquarian passion, among the minutiae of a distant past.

This last danger Professor Barraclough considers to be the widespread and fateful consequence of historicism. I shall deal in some detail with his conception of historicism as it covers—unlike Professor Popper's conception of it—Dilthey's theory of history. But, first, I shall single out for discussion his charge that it leads to pedantry and antiquarianism. His point I take to be this; the sense of the unique in history, the recognition that individual events or periods have intrinsic value, meaning and interest, the conviction that periods must be understood as centred upon themselves, has led the historicists into pedantry, excessive specialization and the unearthing of more and more minute details for their own sake. This view is contradicted by the following facts.

Firstly, the thinkers associated with historicism, Dilthey among them, have combined their belief in the intrinsic interest of historical periods with the aim of grasping these in a wider context—ultimately in the context of universal history. We have just noted Dilthey's stress on the importance of tracing chains of consequences from the past down to the present. Thus the tendency towards minute specialization is in no way based on their professed programme.

Secondly, it is the application—admittedly by historicists, but by no means by them alone—of certain modes of historical research such as the use of archives, rather than any theories, which have led to growing professionalism.

Thirdly, the professionalism and specialization, which, no doubt, has grown up, must be attributed to widespread tendencies of the present age rather than to any theory about history. These tendencies operate everywhere in society, in industrial production, chemical research, the building of ships and medical treatment. Everywhere more precise techniques and a growing body of knowledge make such specialization necessary. In addition, the conditions under which historical research takes place must be taken into account. There are fewer 'amateur' historians who bring a wide experience of public life to their writing and most historical research is conducted by research students aiming at a degree or university lecturers whose careers may depend on the rapid production of papers or monographs produced with scholarly precision.

In turning to the problem of 'historicism' we are coming to grips with the broad philosophical framework of Dilthey's theory of history, though he himself was not very concerned to attach a label to his theories. Historicism, as defined by Professor Barraclough—in its usual and conventional meaning—describes an important historical movement which flourished particularly in the nineteenth century and has recent and contemporary historians among its adherents and sympathizers (c.f. for instance, Professor Powicke's book, *Modern Historians and the Study of History*).

This definition is characterized by the assumption that 'the whole of reality is one vast historical process . . . the nature of everything which exists is, so to say, in its historical development'.

Before entering upon the discussion of this theory two points of explanation may be useful. Firstly, as the historicists were primarily concerned with human history and not, for instance, with physics or chemistry, it is, I think, legitimate to narrow down the definition by reading 'the whole of human reality' and 'everything human' for 'the whole of reality' and 'everything'. The larger claim is not, thereby, surrendered; for historicists, Dilthey among them, believed that physical reality can only be known through human life, that is, in terms of human experiences and thoughts. But, as I am not concerned with a comprehensive theory of knowledge, I am avoiding this wider issue.

Secondly, the concept of development must not be identified with a purposive or teleological process or even with a notion of progress. It simply describes a continuity of change in which later events are affected by earlier ones in a cumulative process.

To understand the nature of historicism we must make a clear distinction between the theory about the methods and scope of history which it advances and the claim to absolute and exclusive priority over all methods of comprehending reality which it makes for this approach. This absolute claim for a subject or method characterizes most 'isms' and marks the transition from a methodology to a philosophy or Weltanschauung. (Thus materialism is the conviction that *only* material objects are real or important and psychologism is the belief in the epistemological priority of psychological methods.) I emphasize this distinction between the historicist methodology and its inflation into a general philosophic position, because critics have attacked the former though their quarrel was really with the latter.

It is the historicist theory of history rather than its Weltanschauung which concerns us here and I shall deal with it first. It is a theory which arose, largely, from the desire of practising historians to extend the range of their subject and to purify its methods and make them more efficient.

As regards, firstly, the range of the subject, historicists claimed that everything human beings have done, thought, believed and produced is accessible to historical treatment and that the field of historical study is, therefore, the whole of human reality in time. On this claim they based their practice and extended their research beyond the traditional preoccupations of historians to, for instance, cultural and social trends and the life of ordinary people in different ages. In this spirit they dealt with religions and philosophic systems, legal codes and moral principles as historical phenomena conditioned by the circumstances under which they arose. No phenomena of the human world could be exempted from this historical treatment and reserved for the exclusive province of some other study such as theology, economics or moral philosophy. This claim, which seems to me perfectly legitimate, must not be confused with the claim of historicism as a Weltanschauung. It is plainly true that the historian can, and must, deal with such facts as that certain religious or moral views were held by certain people at a certain time, that their emergence was conditioned by certain factors and that their acceptance affected the course of events in a certain way. This does not involve the historian in moral valuations or theological judgements of his own, or oblige him to take sides. Having studied evidence of the usual kind he can discover, for instance, that the Greeks of the fifth century B.C. by and large, thought slavery natural and right and this will help him to understand other features of that civilization, say the lack of interest in machinery and other labour saving devices.

The rejection of all external limits to the application of a method of research is not peculiar to history. The psychologist, too, assumes that all mental process can be explained in terms of psychological principles and refuses to exclude religious experiences or the growth of conscience from his scrutiny. The biologist works on the assumption that all a person does, even his thinking out of metaphysical theories, is based on physiological processes in that person's body. All these claims or assumptions are perfectly justified as heuristic principles and do not even clash with each other. The psychologist need not be an atheist nor the biologist a materialist. The biologist, the psychologist, the historian and, for that matter, the theologian and the moral philosopher, need not protect their spheres from each other because these are not defined in terms of an area of reality but by the point of view from which the subject matter is approached. Only on the level of the Weltanschauungen does the clash occur.

If we turn, secondly, to the historicist's concern with the purification of historical methods, we note, above all, a rejection of all rigid unhistorical concepts, all fixed starting points outside history. To avoid the use of unhistorical concepts we have to scrutinize our whole terminology. We have to learn that such apparently simple concepts as piety, love, justice, as well as such concepts as democracy, capitalism, feudalism and even human nature have described different things at different times and may, indeed, have their own history. Only in their proper historical context can they be understood.

As far as the rejection of starting points outside history, or of unhistorical frameworks for the writing of history, is concerned, this is directed against forms of historiography which treat their subject matter as a basis for moral lessons about the wickedness of autocracy and so on, or as illustrations of the unfolding of a divine plan. It is also directed against a view which takes the values and achievements of the present as absolute and treats the past as mere stages in the progress towards it. This, surely, is the point of the historicist's insistence which we have discussed before 'that the past exists for itself' and that ages are centred upon themselves.

Put positively, this last point means that the point of view which he brings to the study of his subject is itself historically relative and conditioned and at the same time not wholly escapable. How, then, can he achieve historical objectivity?

As one side of this problem the question of the moral involvement of the historian has been frequently raised. Two distinct arguments have been offered for the inevitable moral involvement of the historian. Firstly, and this is a point which, for instance, Professor Berlin makes insistently in his 'Historical Inevitability'—when we talk about human beings, consider their actions, enter into their motives and decide on their responsibility for fateful consequences to others, we cannot but involve ourselves in moral judgements. The very language we use to talk about human actions is, in contrast to scientific terminology, fraught with moral implications.

54

Dilthey, who, in this as in the other points discussed, consistently represents the historicist's viewpoint, has dealt with this problem specifically. The moral convictions of an age under consideration are, as we have already seen, intrinsic to its study. They influenced actions and determined their reception by contemporaries. The intrusion of the historian's own moral views can only obscure these issues. (If, for instance, we condemn for homosexuality a person who lived in an age when homosexual practices were commonly accepted, we simply submerge all distinctions of virtue and vice in that age). Once the historian has ascertained the responsibility of a historical agent for certain actions and the consequences of these actions, anybody who is so minded can submit them to moral judgements. But this has nothing to do with history. The historian can escape this human impulse towards moral judgements by the realization that he cannot reach men long dead with his praise or condemnation, cannot call them to repentance, reform, or resistance to evil. If it is, as I believe, the function of moral judgements to guide actions, such moral judgements would be functionless. Thus the historian can acquire detachment through the awareness of historical distance.

But, to turn to the second argument, the historian is a man of his age and has moral and political convictions of his own which he wishes to persuade his contemporaries to accept. If he wants to affect his own time the temptation to draw moral lessons from history, to show the virtues of free enterprise or socialist planning, the value of democracy or of aristocratic government, is strong. Here, Dilthey appreciated, was a dangerous bias which affects not only the historian but all who are concerned with human affairs, the economist, the sociologist or the psychologist. The only counter to this is the historian's or psychologist's scientific training in detachment and objectivity, the exercise of the historical imagination which keeps the variety of moral viewpoints before his eyes and critical awareness of the possibility of bias. The only protection is a tradition of disciplined research and the conviction, shared by historians and their readers, that only history which presents itself as objective and detached can hope to exercise an important influence. What, then, about the less tangible and all the more insidious influences which slant the historian's vision—the intellectual climate, the unspoken presuppositions and assumptions, the preoccupations of his own period? It is the very consciousness of their presence, the realization of the historical relativity of all points of view, which protects us from blind prejudice and unreasoning bias. We may add that it is proper, useful and, indeed, necessary that history should be rewritten from the point of view of each age. In such rewriting, accompanied by a proper awareness of the bias which underlies it, an age becomes critically conscious both of the past and the present.

The programme of historicism as a historical method is, then, an empirical and undogmatic approach to the multiplicity of factors and their varied interrelations in history. It tries to understand the processes of history without any theoretical superstructures and is accompanied by the awareness that those who try to understand the historical course of events are themselves historical beings embedded in that course. It is committed to an explanation, in historical terms, of all that pertains to human life. Insofar as this implies determinism, it is only a methodological assumption shared by other disciplines such as psychology, physiology or economics, concerned to explain human behaviour. The paradox that we appear both conditioned and yet moral, responsible agents, that we are caught up in a web of limiting circumstances and yet have the sense of shaping our destinies freely, is part of our conception of the human condition; it has not arisen through historicism and is not disposed of by its rejection.

The programme of historicism certainly rejects the influence of absolute religious, philosophical or moral points of view on historical reasearch; but it does not deny them their proper sphere. The historicist historian need not believe that the historical approach is the only possible approach to human problems.

But then historicists proceeded—in a way which is psychologically understandable and which is familiar to the student of the history of ideas—to interpret their methodological principles as ultimate metaphysical truths about reality. They proceeded that is, to the belief that theirs was the only proper approach.

Historicism as a Weltanschauung does, indeed, carry alarming implications, for it raises the spectre of relativism which leads to nihilism. Our lives, in the personal, social and political spheres, demand constant actions and decisions based on clear convictions, moral ideals and principles. But, if every religion, every philosophy, every moral system is tainted with relativity, merely the product of the strains and stresses, the hopes and intentions of an age, how is decisive action based on independent moral conviction, possible? Are we not condemned to sceptical inactivity, or, worse still, are we not tempted into a type of higher opportunism, into bowing down before the forces which seem to be carried vigorously by the tendencies of history? Could this, perhaps, have been the very 'trahison des clercs' of the German scholars in the face of Hitler's rise, or of intellectuals of various countries in the face of triumphant communism?

This has, quite obviously, been the source of a widespread recoil from historicism and of a renewed insistence on the importance of moral values. Professor Carr, for instance, refers (in *The New Society*) to the necessity for 'aims and purposes which will ultimately be derived from values which have their source outside history'. Professor Barraclough, too, speaks about the need for 'some constructive purpose, some criterion of value'. (I have already quoted his references to an 'end outside history' and 'a new set of values' which occur in the same context.) He would have been on stronger ground if he had stressed the independent importance of values. It is legitimate and, indeed, necessary to insist that when the historian wishes to apply his historical knowledge to practical purposes in his own world he must do so on the basis of principles which are moral and not merely historical. He can hardly be described as a full human being unless he possesses such moral principles. But Professor Barraclough wants, it appears, to introduce these ends outside history and new values into historical research itself and on this point the historicist's case is strong.

57

Dilthey himself was deeply and anxiously concerned with the problem of moral scepticism which historicism as a philosophy raises. He uses, essentially, two distinct lines of argument to reconcile the historicist position with his own serious moral and political concern. The first, though characteristic of his general philosophic position, falls, I think, outside the framework of the necessary assumptions of historicism as defined above. I shall not, therefore, attempt to argue it out though, in fairness, it should be briefly stated. The second I consider to be part of the historicist's case.

Dilthey's first line of argument is rooted in his moral theory which must be described as naturalistic. He believed that values arose through, and only through, acts of valuing by human agents. Valuable thus means valued by somebody. If something is valued for its own sake it is an intrinsic value (or has intrinsic value); if it is valued as a means of achieving something else it is an instrumental value (or has instrumental value). Because each human being values his life unconditionally and for its own sake, the individual's life constitutes an intrinsic value. Furthermore, because human beings throughout history and through all changes of value-systems agree in valuing their own existence, it constitutes a universal, or objective, value. Thus, in accordance with this theory, the intrinsic and objective value of individuals is not a metaphysical assumption but an expression of the fact that all men value their lives for their own sakes. Because all other things have been considered as valuable only insofar as they maintained, protected, furthered and enriched human life, human beings themselves constitute the sole objective value which is unaffected by the flux of history and the change of moral standards. Respect for individuality is the anchorage of moral judgements and is not subject to historical relativity.

To discuss this theory on its merits is beyond the scope of this book. It should only be pointed out that Dilthey's liberal and humanistic belief in the intrinsic value of individuals is, as it were, the counterpart to his conviction that individuals are the only real units of history and that understanding of them provides the key to the interpretation of history. There is a certain consistency of outlook in Dilthey's emphasis on the individual in both the moral and the historical sphere. But there is, of course, no logical connection between the moral and the historical theories. The one does not follow from the other and either could be held independently.

The moral imperative to respect human beings (by whatever steps it may have been arrived at from the fact that human beings value their own existence) implies, of course, the freedom of those to whom it is directed. Dilthey's second line of argument is concerned with the historicist's attitude to the problem of freedom. It consists of a counter attack on the belief in timelessly fixed moral codes and static eternal values. Such a belief denies the true freedom and creativity of man. We give proper recognition to these essential, human characteristics only by showing that man, finding himself in varying circumstances and concretely conditioned by them, can subjectively and freely, interpret these, appreciate new values and set himself new purposes. Responding to the conditions of our time and influenced by the past, we yet create the incalculably new. The relativity of values is only the reverse of the coin of man's creative freedom. For this reason history is not the orchestration of an eternally fixed theme, but the story of the creative struggle of man to come to terms with reality.

Existentialists, in particular, have adopted and developed this point of Dilthey's and they, in turn, have influenced modern thinkers, especially theologians. An example, accessible to English readers, of a contemporary adaptation of Dilthey's argument is contained in R. Bultmann's broadcast, 'The Quest for Meaning in History', (printed in the *Listener*, September 1, 1955).

9. THE USES OF HISTORY

Man strives for knowledge for its own sake and, therefore, historical research needs as little justification in terms of its practical uses as physics does in terms of its technological applications. Yet every class of knowledge is the knowledge of something and throws a beam of light on a particular sphere of reality. To ask, therefore, about the use or function of a discipline is to ask about the area it illuminates. In this sense history certainly has its uses. It helps us, first of all, to understand the society of which we are members, the tradition to which we are heir, the institutions we serve, the laws we obey—in fact, the world we live in—by tracing the way in which the past has brought about the present. Because this backward glance also takes in the genesis of our own convictions it helps us to gain a critical attitude towards our own civilization. But perhaps the most important function of history is to illuminate human nature. The story of man's actions in time reveals the range of his potentialities and thus teaches us what man is. History, fulfilling these functions widens our horizon and provides a liberal education. But has it not also more practical uses? After all, throughout the ages human beings have looked to history for predictions of what was likely to happen, by means of which the future could be controlled. We have noted voices of discontent with a purely contemplative history and the demand that history should serve some end or purpose. If it could prepare us for the future that would indeed provide it with some practical purpose. If we cannot class history as a science and if we have to reject the notion of historical laws governing the succession of facts, we have no basis for establishing long-term predictions with any certainty. Yet it has seemed reasonable to historians to assume that it was one of the functions of history 'to cast' in Professor Carr's words 'a beam of the past over the issues which dominate present and future'. Indeed eminent historians—Jakob Burckhardt is a striking example—have, out of the wealth of their historical knowledge, made shrewd forecasts of the shape of things to come.

On this issue Dilthey took up a moderate and reasonable position. There are certainly some regularities and some continuity in history. There are characteristic ways in which things happen and interaction takes place but, because men are free and creative, no certain predictions can be based on them.

Therefore, the way in which historical knowledge aided the anticipation of the future was, he believed, analogous to that in which experience aided—in a logically not entirely analysable form—judgement in many spheres of life. This is illustrated by the fact that, though schoolchildren are different and new problems arise daily in teaching them, ten years of teaching experience can equip a man with the capacity to deal efficiently with new problems as they arise. Even more apt may be the analogy to the sphere of art and literature. The historical actor gains from the knowledge of history precisely as much guidance as the practitioner of any creative art from the history of his subject. The writing, for instance, of good poetry and the judging of it as good, depends on familiarity with poetry, that is, on knowledge of the history of poetry. Of course the contemplation of the past of poetry is not sufficient equipment for the writing of a good poem which can never be a mere imitation, or for the judgement of it, which can never be a mere application of a rigid standard. Nor can we predict future developments by projecting tendencies of the past. Yet, by steeping ourselves in the history of poetry, we nourish our creative powers, sharpen our judgement and become sensitive to new developments. It is in this way that the contemplation of history aids our judgement of the present and our power to take effective action for the future.

In the preceding pages I have tried to sketch the outlines of Dilthey's theory of history and to show its relevance to contemporary discussions on the nature and functions of history. Dilthey's approach is characterized by sturdy empiricism. 'Immerse yourself wholly,' he said once in a lecture to his students, 'in this sense of reality.' He rejected, therefore, any kind of metaphysical construction and refused to bring to the study of the facts any rigid rationalistic, theological or moral assumptions. But the reality he was concerned with was not just the world of physical facts; it was the human world which he saw suffused throughout with meaning arising from the consciousness, feeling, purposes and valuations of human beings. He therefore contrasted his carefully worked out theories of understanding and interpretation with the procedures of the natural sciences. What man has done, thought and created, he believed, man can understand. By extending our understanding both to individuals, who are the only real units in history and to the man-made—and, therefore, comprehensible—contexts in which they stand, we grasp the historical world as meaningful. By thus recapturing not some metaphysical meaning but the meaning which individuals, here and there, have perceived in and attributed to their circumstances, the meaning which informed their actions and became embodied in their creations, the historian can tell a meaningful story.

Outlines and summaries such as those given here can, of course, not do full justice to the work of a great thinker. It remains, therefore, to let Dilthey speak in his own words.

NOTE

Volume VII of the collected works of Dilthey was edited in 1926 by B. Groethuysen, one of his disciples and collaborators. Some of the material is taken from the published proceedings of the Prussian Academy of the Sciences, but the bulk is an editorial arrangement—sometimes based on hints from Dilthey—of a mass of manuscripts and dictation.

Part I (pages 3—78 of Vol. VII) called 'Studies towards the Foundations of the Human Studies' contains three preliminary studies of which only the first was ever published (Proceedings of the Prussian Academy of the Sciences 1905). The others are notes which probably served as a basis for other papers read to the Academy.

Part II (pages 79—188 of Vol. VII) entitled 'The Construction of the Historical World in the Human Studies' was read to the Prussian Academy in January 1910 and published in their proceedings in December 1910.

Part III (pages 191—291 of Vol. VII) described by the editor as the 'Plan for the Continuation of the Construction of the Historical World in the Human Studies' is called 'Drafts towards a critique of Historical Reason'. The completion of the work on the lines of these manuscripts would probably have involved a rewriting and re-arranging of Part II. This probably dates from the period 1907-1910.

Part IV (pages 295—347 of Vol. VII) is called 'Appendix'

and contains earlier, rejected versions of sections of parts one and two.

Only four fairly short quotations from Parts I and IV are included in my translation. Parts II and III seem to me to contain the most important material and substantial portions from both are given.

After the page reference of each quotation I have given the part and the title of the section from which it is taken.

CHAPTER I

THE HISTORICAL WORLD AND
THE METHODS OF HISTORY

EDITOR'S INTRODUCTION

The selection of passages in this chapter attempts to indicate the broad sweep of Dilthey's approach. From it should emerge how Dilthey used his key terms such as 'the historical world', 'life', 'meaning', 'expression', 'understanding', and 'interpretation', (hermeneutics).

This historical world, the subject matter of history, is life in its temporal extension. The word 'life'—and this is crucial for the understanding of the text—is, for Dilthey, a terminus technicus. By it he refers to the whole sphere of human life, its manifestations, creations and ramifications. 'Life' is the life of mankind with its social organizations and cultural achievements. It does not represent an emphasis on the biological features of man which he shares with other animals. In fact animals or plants as such, are, in this sense, not part of life at all.

History is, thus, concerned with what human beings have done and suffered in the course of time, how they have organized themselves, how institutions arose and how they, in turn, affected human beings. It is not concerned, in this usage, with purely physical events in time, such as the formation of the earth's crust, except insofar as these have affected human beings.

These initial definitions provided Dilthey with the basis for answering the epistemological question—how is historical knowledge possible? Put briefly the answer is this; human minds can understand history because they are dealing with what other human minds have done and created. Dilthey, therefore, goes on to ask—what are the common features of human life, which we can use for the understanding of historical processes?

Dilthey's concept of meaning we have already discussed in the introduction. Here we need only reiterate briefly that he believed that 'life' was characterized throughout by being meaningful. It is meaningful in terms of the various relations in which things stand to us or to each other. Though there is nothing like 'the meaning' of history, the situations with which the historian deals are already meaningful, that is, they have received interpretations from the people involved in them.

How, then, do we discover the meaning situations have, or have had for others? In answer to this question Dilthey developed his theory of expressions and the understanding and interpreting of them.

By an expression Dilthey means the outer sign, consisting of an event in the physical world, of something inner, that is, something in a person's mind, such as a thought or a feeling. A sign can be conventional or natural. A word is the former, a cry of pain the latter. Cutting across this classification there is another which divides signs into those which are intentional, that is, are used to convey meaning, and those which are not Literary works, for instance, are purely intentional signs; their purpose is communication. But man's actions are unintentional signs. A person mowing the lawn does not try to communicate anything yet he clearly conveys to the spectator 'what is in his mind'. Some signs may convey, both intentionally and unintentionally, a meaning to others. For instance, a letter may, intentionally, inform me of something or other and, at the same time, convey that the writer does not like me, or is depressed, or whatever the case may be.

Various means of understanding these expressions or signs are at our disposal. We recognize natural signs, the relation between pain and tears, let us say, from our own experience. We understand conventional signs from having learned the convention. In the case of actions, which are also often conventional in the sense that there are accepted ways of doing things, we understand them by being familiar with that

E   65

sphere of life. (A bushman might not understand what the man was doing with his lawn-mower.) In many cases we understand by relating the sign to a wider context, the whole work of an author, the trend of the conversation, what we know about a person. In that case, in particular, we speak of interpretation, or what Dilthey, following Schleiermacher, called Hermeneutics.

By these means we come to understand individuals, their productions and, also, the wider contexts, such as communities and cultural organizations in which individuals stand. The goal of this understanding is always penetration to the mental states or processes which lie behind outer manifestations and we are helped towards this not merely by purely intellectual processes but by the wealth of our own experience of life.

The fact that, in history and indeed, in the human studies altogether, we are grasping what is, in principle, akin to us, distinguishes these from the natural sciences and gives the human studies a particular advantage. But this is counterbalanced by a particular difficulty; the strong pull of practical life constantly endangers objectivity in the judgement of human affairs and, however much we may strive to detach ourselves from this pull, we are apt to remain bound by the horizon of our age, nation and class. Only insight into these processes can help us to overcome this bias.

TEXT

Page 278. Part III. The Problem of History
We are, first of all, historical beings and, after that, contemplators of history; only because we are the one do we become the other . . .

I am involved in the interactions of society because its various systems[1] intersect in my life. These systems have sprung from the same human nature as I experience in myself and understand in others. The language in which I think and my concepts originated in the course of time. Thus,

[1] By these systems Dilthey means, as we shall see, economic life, education, etc.

to impenetrable depths within myself, I am a historical being. The fact that the investigator of history is the same as the one who makes it, is the first condition which makes scientific history possible; here we have the first significant element for the solution of the epistemological problem of history.

Page 254. Part III. The Approach to World History
Throughout history a living, active, creative and responsive soul is present at all times and places. Every first class document is an expression of such a soul. That these documents are so scarce for a certain period results from the selection which history, in the form of memory, makes from the piles of what is written. It allows all that has no meaning to fall to dust, ashes and rags.

Page 191. Part III. The Task of a Critique of Historical Reason
The connections in the mind-affected world arise in the human subject and it is the effort of the mind to determine the systematic meaning of that world which links the individual logical processes involved to each other. Thus, on the one hand, the comprehending subject creates this mind-affected world and, on the other, tries to gain objective knowledge of it. Hence we face the problem, how does the mental construction of the mind-affected world make knowledge of mind-affected reality possible? Earlier I have described this task as a critique of historical reason. The task can only be accomplished if the individual processes, which work together in the creation of this system, can be sorted out and it can be shown what part each of them plays, firstly, in the construction of the historical course of events in the mind-affected world and, secondly, in the discovery of its systematic nature. In what follows we shall see how far the difficulties inherent in the mutual dependence of specific truths can be dissolved and how the real principle of comprehension in the human studies can be gradually deduced from experience. Understanding is the rediscovery of the I in the Thou; the mind rediscovers itself at ever higher levels of connectedness; this sameness of the mind in the I and the Thou and in every

subject of a community, in every system of culture and, finally, in the totality of mind and universal history, makes the working together of the different processes in the human studies possible. In these the knowing subject is one with its object, which is the same at all stages of its objectification.

Pages 79-85. Part II. The Delimitation of the Human Studies

Side by side with the natural sciences a group of studies linked together by their common subject matter has grown naturally from the problems of life itself. These include history, economics, law, politics and psychology and the study of religion, literature, poetry, architecture, music and philosophic world views and systems. All these studies refer to the same great fact; mankind, which they describe, recount and judge and about which they form concepts and theories . . .

In the studies listed the subjects of assertions vary in comprehensiveness from individuals, families, composite associations, nations, ages, historical movements or evolutionary series, social organizations, systems of culture and other sections of the whole of humanity, to humanity itself. These can be talked about and described and theories can be developed about them; but they always refer to the same fact, humanity or human-social-historical reality. Thus it is possible to define this group of disciplines as having a reference to the same fact, humanity, and to separate them from the natural sciences. In addition, because of this common reference, assertions about the logical subjects comprised in the fact, humanity, support each other. The two great classes of disciplines listed, the study of history (including the description of the contemporary state of society) and the systematic human studies, are, throughout, dependent on each other and form a solid whole . . .

In these studies a tendency, inherent in the subject matter itself, is at work. The study of language embraces the physiology of the speech organs as well as the teaching of the meaning of words and sentences. The chemical effects of gunpowder are as much part of the course of a modern war as the moral qualities of the soldiers who stand in its smoke. But, in the nature of the group of disciplines with which we are dealing there is a tendency, which develops more and more strongly as they advance, to relegate the physical side of events to the role of conditions and means of comprehension. This is the turning towards self-knowledge, the movement of understanding from the external to the internal. This tendency makes use of every expression of life in order to understand the mental content from which it arises. In history we read of productive labour, settlements, wars, foundations of states. They fill our souls with great images and tell us about the historical world which surrounds us; but what moves us, above all, in these accounts is what is inaccessible to the senses and can only be experienced inwardly; it is inherent in the outer events which originate from it and which, in turn, react on it. This tendency does not depend upon an external point of view from which life is surveyed; it is founded directly on it. For all that is valuable in life is contained in what can be experienced and the whole outer clamour of history circles around it; in it goals of which nature is ignorant arise. Here the will strives to achieve development and form. Only in the world of the mind which, active, responsible and self-determined, moves within us and, in it alone, has life its value, its goal and its meaning . . .

In the human studies we are dealing with states, churches, institutions, customs, books and works of art; in such facts, as in man himself, there is always the reference from an outer sensuous side to one withdrawn from the senses, and, therefore, inner.

We must now determine what this inner side is. It is a common error to identify our knowledge of this inner side with the course of mental life, that is, with psychology. I shall try to eliminate the error by making the following points.

The apparatus of law books, judges, litigants, defendants, as it manifests itself at a certain time and place is, in the first instance, the expression of a purposive system of regulations which gives it its impetus. This purposive system is directed towards an unambiguous external regulation of individual wills; it created the conditions for the perfect life as far as they can be realized by compulsion and delimits the power spheres of individuals in relation to each other, to things and to the general will. The law must, therefore, take the form of imperatives backed by the power of a community to enforce them. Thus, historical understanding of the law in force in a certain community at a given time can be achieved by going back from the outer apparatus to this source in the mind, that is, to the system of legal imperatives produced by the collective will and enforced by it. Ihering[1] discusses the spirit of Roman law in this way. His understanding of this spirit is not psychological insight. It is achieved by going back to a mind-created structure with a pattern and law of its own. Legal science, from the interpretation of a passage in the Corpus Juris to the understanding of the whole Roman law and thence to the comparison of legal systems, is based on this. Hence, is subject matter is not identical with the outer facts and occurrences through and in which the law takes its course. These facts are the concern of legal science only in so far as they embody the law. The capture of the criminal, the illness of witnesses, or the apparatus of execution belong, as such, to pathology and technical science.

It is the same with aesthetics. The work of a poet lies in front of me. It consists of letters, is put together by compositors and printed by machines. But literary history and criticism are only concerned with what the pattern of words refers to, not—and this is decisive—with the processes in the poet's mind but with a structure created by these processes yet separable from them. The structure of a drama lies in its particular combination of subject, poetic mood, plot and means of presentation. Each of these elements performs its function in the structure of the work; and these functions are related to each other by a law intrinsic to poetry. Thus the primary subject matter of literary history or criticism is wholly distinct from the mental processes of the poet or his readers. A mind-created structure is realized and enters the

---

[1] Rudolf von Ihering, 1818-1892. Leading German theoretician of Jurisprudence, author of *The Spirit of the Roman Law in the Different Stages of its Development*.

world of the senses; we can understand it only by penetrating behind that world.

Pages 86-87. Part II.   The Delimitation of the Human Studies
If we consider mankind only in terms of perception and knowledge it would be merely a physical fact for us and, as such, could only be explained in terms of the natural sciences. But, insofar as man experiences human states, gives expression to his experience and understands the expressions, mankind becomes the subject of the human studies. The interrelation of life, expression and understanding, embraces gestures, facial expressions and words by which men communicate with each other, permanent mental creations revealing the profundity of the creator to the man who can grasp it, and permanent objectifications of the mind in social structures in which human nature is surely and for ever manifest.

Even the psycho-physical unit, man, knows himself through the same mutual relationship of expression and understanding; he becomes aware of himself in the present; he recognizes himself in memory as something that once was; but, when he tries to hold fast and grasp his states of mind by turning his attention upon himself, then the narrow limits of such an introspective method of self-knowledge show themselves; only his actions, his formulated expressions of life and the effects of these on others, teach man about himself. Thus, he comes to know himself only by the circuitous route of understanding. What we once were, how we developed and became what we are, we learn from the way we acted, from the plans for our lives we once made, from how we pursued a profession, from old, forgotten letters, from judgements made on us long ago. Briefly, it is through the process of understanding that life gains illumination about its depths and yet we understand ourselves and others only by putting what we have actually experienced into every kind of expression of our own and others' lives. So, mankind becomes the subject matter of the human studies only because the relation between experience, expression and understanding exists. The human studies are thus based on the relationship which provides their distinctive criterion. A discipline belongs to the human studies only when its subject matter becomes accessible to us through the procedure which is founded on the connection between life, expression and understanding.

Pages 131-132. Part II. Life
Thus, the development of the human studies depends on the deepening of experience and on the increasing tendency to bring their content to the surface; at the same time it is dependent on the spread of understanding over all the objectifications of mind[1] and on the increasingly complete and methodical extraction of the mental content from the different expressions of life.

What we grasp in experience and understanding is life as the context which embraces mankind. When we first face this great fact which, for us, is not only the starting point of the human studies but also of philosophy, we must try to get behind the scientific elaboration of it and grasp it in its raw state.

Thus the life peculiar to man shows distinctive characteristics in its individual aspects such as relations, attitudes, conduct, the shaping of things and people and the suffering caused by them. On the stable basis from which the differentiated processes arise there is nothing which does not contain a vital relationship to the I. As everything is related to it the state of the I changes constantly, according to the things and people around it. There is not a person or a thing which is only an object to me; for me it involves pressure or advancement, the goal of some striving or a restriction of my will, importance, demand for consideration, inner closeness or resistance, distance or strangeness. Through the life relationship, either transitory or permanent, these people and things bring me happiness, expand my existence or heighten my powers; or they confine the scope of my life, exercise pressure on me and drain my strength. The attributes which things thus acquire only in the life-relationship to me produce resultant changes in my state. Thus, on the basis of life itself types of behaviour arise, such as perceiving, evaluating and the setting

[1] Books, laws and institutions are such objectifications.

of purposes, with countless nuances merging into each other. In the course of life they form systematic connections which embrace and determine all activity and development.

Pages 261-262. Part III. The Possibility of Objective Knowledge in the Human Studies

The problem of how objective knowledge is possible in the human studies goes back to the question of how it can be realized in history. How is history possible? This way of formulating the question already implies a concept of history. We have seen that this concept is dependent on that of life. Historical life is part of the whole of life which is given in experience and understanding. Life in this sense, therefore, extends over the whole range of objective mind accessible to experience. Life is the fundamental fact which must form the starting point for philosophy. It is that which is known from within, that behind which we cannot go. Life cannot be brought before the judgement seat of reason. Life seen as a temporal succession of events which affect each other is historical life. It is only possible to grasp it through the reconstruction of the course of events in a memory which reproduces not the particular event but the system of connections and the stages of its development. What memory accomplishes when it surveys the course of a life is achieved in history by linking together the expressions of life which have become part of the objective mind, according to their temporal and dynamic relationships. This is history . . .

Historical objectivity is only possible if, among the many points of view from which history can be seen as a coherent whole of distinguishable parts, there is one from which a series of events can be recaptured as it happened.[1]

First of all I shall introduce the concept of meaning. The connectedness of history is that of life itself, integrated under the conditions of its natural environment. A part has meaning for the whole to which it belongs only if it is linked to it by a relationship found in life; for it is not intrinsic to the relation of whole and part that the part should have a meaning

[1] Here Dilthey is referring to Ranke's often quoted aim to show 'what it was really like'.

for the whole. In this lies what appears to be an insoluble riddle. We must construct the whole from its parts and, yet, the whole must contain the reason for the meaning given to the part and for the place assigned to it.[1] We have already seen that the mainspring of historical work is the mutual dependence of conclusions reached, in this case interdependence of whole and part. History must teach what life is; yet, because it is the course of life in time, history is dependent on life and derives its content from it.

There would be a simple escape from this circle if there were unconditional norms, purposes or values, against which historical contemplation and comprehension could be measured.

History itself produces principles which are valid because they make the relations contained in life explicit. Such principles are the obligation which is based on a contract and the recognition of the dignity and value of every individual simply as a man. These truths are universally valid because they impart order to every aspect of the historical world.

Page 237. Part III. Meaning and Structure
Experience in its concrete reality is made coherent by the category of meaning. This is the unity which, through memory, joins together what has been experienced either directly or through empathy. Its meaning does not lie in something outside the experiences which gives them unity but is contained in them and constitutes the connections between them.

This system of connections is, thus, the peculiar form of relatedness, or category, found in all that can be experienced.

Where the meaning of the life of an individual, of myself, of another, or of a nation, lies, is not clearly determined by the fact that there is such a meaning. That it is there is always certain to the person remembering it as a series of related experiences. Only in the last moment of a life can the balance

[1] To understand the House of Lords fully we must know about its members; what it is to be a member is understood by knowing about the House of Lords. A lord who takes no part in the work of the House has no meaning for it.

74

of its meaning be struck so it can be done only for a moment, or by another who retraces that life.

Thus Luther's life receives its meaning from the fact that it connects all the concrete events in which the new religiousness was embraced and established. This, then, forms a section in the more comprehensive concrete context of what occurred before and afterwards. Here meaning is seen in a historical form. But one can also seek this meaning in the positive values of life. Then it stands in a relation to subjective feelings.[1].

Page 240. Part III. Meaning, Significance and Value
The significance which a fact receives as a fixed link in the meaning of the whole is a relation in life and not an intellectual one, not an insertion of reason or thought into a part of the event. The significance emerges from life itself.

Pages 319-322. Part IV. How is Knowledge Possible in the Human Studies? (German editor's title).
A significant complement to experience, through which, alone, we can know the abundance and continuity of mental life, lies in the fact that inner states find outward expressions and that the latter can be understood by going back to the former.

An outer manifestation is the expression of an inner state by means of an artificial convention or a natural, ordered relationship between expression and what is expressed. In both cases it is the outward sign of a fact.

The former relation holds good even when the sign, meaning the presence of one fact, apparently only signifies that another, outer fact is present. Even here understanding takes place for, by means of the sign, factual knowledge is communicated from the consciousness of A to that of B on the basis of an artificial convention. That a train approaches the station and that a signal is given are two external facts but an agreement about their connection establishes an inner relation between a communicating mind and the one that understands; only in this way does the one outer event be-

---

[1] Love of poetry, for instance, is such a subjective feeling; it constitutes a positive value and so gives meaning to life.

come a sign for the other. It is different with those signs which are the natural expressions of mental content and thus indicate it.

Here we must, first of all, distinguish the relationship between the mental content and the actions which alter facts or produce lasting institutions. Actions and their permanent, outward results constantly help us to reconstruct the mental content from which they arose. The civil law was created in order to regulate the life of a certain period but the student of the age of Frederick uses it to understand the spirit of that age; he goes back from the laws to the intentions of the legislator and from there back to the spirit from which they arose. Thus, from examining institutions we understand the mental content which, in the form of social values, purposes and consciousness of obligation, was present at a certain time and place and which expressed itself in these outer manifestations. Then mental content expresses itself for us unintentionally, unwilled; the deeds were done on an upsurge of will, in order to achieve something, not to communicate something to contemporaries or successors. Now they stand as signs of a mental content which once existed, as the remnant which survives.

Quite different from this is the expression of mental content arising from the urge to express it, either to oneself or to others. This is the proper sphere of understanding and its disciplined use in interpretation. It may be the replicas which give us a feeble idea of the Zeus of Phidias, or the Apocalypse of Dürer, or the ninth symphony, a drama or a philosophic system, a poem by Goethe or a scientific masterpiece of Newton's, in fact, either a single creation or a body of concepts, which expresses some fact or other; in all these there is something outward which originated as the expression of a mental content and thus helps towards the understanding of that content.

Deliberate expressions and actions express mental content differently according to the way they enter into outer manifestations. Every action is determined by conditions; their relationship to the living totality of the acting person produces his aims, energy, means and, if the action goes on, his adjustment to circumstances. In consequence, the inference we can draw from it about mental content is limited. We must group actions together. Memoranda, decisions, speeches, in brief, all kinds of expressions which the course of an action demands and which, therefore, spring, not from the need for expression but from the will to be effective, are parts of political action; thus we see in them various correlated results of the activity of the will; when we relate these results to each other they reveal one of the relationships of life itself; the greater the number of situations from which they arise the richer the understanding of the mental content from which they sprang; but they are always only sections, vistas, which show a part of the landscape; never do we see it in all its variety.

I will now call to the reader's mind the quintessence of Goethe's artistic, literary and scientific publications and of his literary remains. How different is the relation between expression and mental content. We can solve the problem of how to understand this; indeed, in a sense, we understand him better that Goethe understood himself . . .

If the poets had only left us accounts of their activity but the poems themselves had perished, how little they would mean to us. We must analyse the poems in order to penetrate to the heart of the poetic process and grasp it in all its fullness . . .

The comprehension of the structure of mental life rests, above all, on the interpretation of the works in which the connections of mental life are completely expressed.

Pages 225-226. Part III. Hermeneutics
Interpretation would be impossible if expressions of life were completely strange. It would be unnecessary if nothing strange were in them. It lies, therefore, between these two extremes. It is always required where something strange is to be grasped through the art of understanding.

Interpretation, pursued for its own sake, without an external practical purpose, already takes place in conversation. Every significant conversation demands that the expression of the speaker should be placed into an inner context which is not given in his words. The better we know the speaker the more we are tempted to trace the concealed movement behind his part in the conversation to its source. And the famous interpreter of the Platonic dialogues[1] emphasizes how valuable such exercises in the interpretation of the spoken word are for the interpretation of the written. Next follows the interpretation of speeches in a debate; after all, they are only fully understood if, from the context of the debate, the political allegiance of the speaker is appreciated, the allusions explained and allowance made for the individual's weakness or strength in the subject under debate.

Pages 134-138. Part II. Ideal Units as the Basis of Life and Experience of it

The lives of individuals are infinitely enriched through their relationship to their environment, to other people and to things. But, every individual is, also, a point where systems intersect; systems which go through individuals, exist within them, but reach beyond their life and possess an independent existence and development of their own through the content, the value, the purpose, which is realized in them. Thus they are subjects of an ideal kind. Some kind of knowledge of reality is inherent in them; standpoints for valuation develop within them, purposes are realized in them; they have a meaning which they sustain in the context of the mind-affected world.

This is already the case in some of the systems of culture, for instance, art and philosophy, in which there is no organization to link the parts. Furthermore, organized associations arise. Thus, economic life creates its own associations; in the case of science research centres come into being; of all cultural systems religions develop the strongest organizations. In the family and in the different intermediate forms between it and the state, as well as in the latter itself, we find the highest development of common goals within a community.

Every organized unit in a state acquires a knowledge of itself, of the rules on which its existence is founded and of its

[1] The German theologian and philosopher, Friedrich Ernst Daniel Schleiermacher, 1768-1834, Dilthey wrote *The Life of Schleiermacher*.

place in the whole. It enjoys the values which have grown up within it; it realizes the purposes, characteristic of it, which maintain and further its existence. It is itself a good of mankind and realizes goods. It has a meaning of its own in the context of mankind.

We have reached the point where society and history unfold before us. But it would be wrong to confine history to the co-operation of human beings for common purposes. The individual person in his own independent existence is a historical being. He is determined by his place in time and space and his position in the interaction of cultural systems and communities. The historian has, therefore, to understand the whole life of an individual as it expresses itself at a certain time and place. It is the whole web of connections which stretches from individuals concerned with their own existence to the cultural systems and communities and, finally, to the whole of mankind, which makes up the character of society and history. Individuals are as much the logical subjects of history as communities and contexts.

Life, experience of life and the human studies are, thus, constantly related and interacting. It is not conceptual procedure which forms the foundation of the human studies but the becoming aware of a mental state in its totality and the rediscovering of it by empathy. Here life grasps life and the power with which these two basic procedures of the human studies are carried out preconditions their adequacy in all their branches.

So, at this point, too, we notice an overall difference between the natural sciences and the human studies. In the first, scientific thinking, the productive achievements of which are esoteric,[1] has become detached from our practical contact with the external world; but, in the human studies, a connection between life and science is retained so that thought arising from life remains the foundation of scientific activity. In certain circumstances life itself succeeds in penetrating its own depths to an extent which surpasses the power of a

[1] The productive achievements of science are theories and these are esoteric in the sense that what we are told about the atomic structure of a table lies outside our daily experience.

79

Carlyle and the understanding of others achieves a virtuosity which even Ranke does not equal. Great religious natures like Augustine and Pascal are the eternal models for insight drawn from personal experience and the court and politics give a training in the art of understanding other people which looks behind outward appearances; a man of action like Bismarck, whose very nature makes him consider his aims whenever he writes a letter or conducts a conversation, cannot be equalled in the art of reading intentions behind expressions by any interpreter of political acts or critic of historical accounts. In many cases there is nothing to choose between a poetically sensitive listener's grasping of a play and the most excellent literary-historical analysis. In the historical and social studies conceptualization, too, is constantly determined by life itself. I am referring to the connection which constantly leads from life and from the forming of concepts about the purposes of existence, destiny, character, passions and values to history as a science. In the period in France in which political activity was based more on understanding people and leading person-alities than on a scientific study of law, economics and the state and when a position in the life of the court was based on this art, literary memoirs and works about character and pas-sions reached a height they have never achieved since; they were produced by people who were very little influenced by the scientific study of psychology and history. Here an inner connection links the observation of high society, the writers, the poets who learn from them, the systematic philosophers and the scientific historians, who are all influenced by poetry and literature. In the beginnings of political science among the Greeks we see how the concepts of political acts and the constitutions within which they occurred developed from political life itself and how new creations in the latter lead to new theories. This whole relation is clearest in the older stages of jurisprudence among the Romans and Teutons.

Thus, the starting point from life and the constant connec-tion with it forms the first fundamental feature in the struc-ture of the human studies; for they rest on experience, under-standing and knowledge of life. This direct relationship in which life and the human studies stand to each other leads, in the latter, to a conflict between the tendencies of life and the scientific goals of the human studies. Because historians, economists, teachers of law and students of religion stand in the midst of life they want to influence it. They subject historical personages, mass movements and tendencies to their judgement, which is conditioned by their individuality, the nation to which they belong and the age in which they live. Even when they believe that their work is not based on pre-suppositions they are determined by their horizon; for every analysis of the concepts of a former generation reveals in them constituents which derive from the presuppositions of that generation. But, in every science as such the demand for general validity is implied. If the human studies are to be sciences in the strict sense of the word they must aim at validity more consciously and more critically.

Many of the scientific divergences which have recently appeared in the logic of the human studies stem from the conflict between these two tendencies. It expresses itself most strongly in the science of history. So I have made it the focal point of this discussion.

Only in the actual construction of the human studies is the conflict settled; but the general statements about the connection between the human studies which follow already contain the principle for this settlement. Here are the conclusions we have reached. Life and experience of it are the ever freshly flowing sources of the understanding of the social-historical world; starting from life, understanding penetrates into ever new depths; only in reacting on life and society do the human studies achieve their highest significance and this is constantly growing. But the road to such effectiveness must pass through the objectivity of scientific knowledge. Men were actively conscious of this in the great creative periods of the human studies. After many distractions due to our national development and to the application of a one-sided ideal of culture since Jakob Burckhardt, we are today filled with the desire to develop this objectivity of the human studies with an open mind, critically and stringently. I find the *principle for the settlement of the conflict* within these studies in the understanding of the historical world as a system of interactions centred on itself; each individual system of interactions contained in it has, through the positing of values and their realization, its centre within itself; but all are structurally linked into a whole in which, from the significance of the individual parts, the meaning of the whole context of the social-historical world arises; thus, every value judgement and every purpose projected into the future, must be based exclusively on this structural context.

CHAPTER II

THE HISTORICAL RELEVANCE OF
AUTOBIOGRAPHY AND BIOGRAPHY

EDITOR'S INTRODUCTION

Understanding, in contrast to knowing, is, in Dilthey's terminology, the process by which we comprehend the individual
phenomena of the human world. Historical understanding,
which has to deal with complex phenomena, may conveniently be approached via the understanding of individual
persons. This we encounter in autobiography—the literary
expression of a person's understanding of his own life—and in
biography—the comprehension of another man's life. Autobiography is, epistemologically speaking, a relatively simple
case of understanding because, in it, a person sees his life as a
meaningful pattern which takes shape in his own experience
and which his own actions, plans and decisions have helped to
produce; he forgets, for instance, what seems unimportant to
him. In biography, too, we have to take into account the
meaning his life had for the person who lived it, the way in
which he himself interpreted the situations which faced him.
We have, therefore, to make use of his diaries, letters,
speeches or published works in which he himself expressed
that meaning. But the advantages of biography over autobiography are that the life under consideration is completed
and can be looked at detachedly and critically.

Biographies not only serve to satisfy intrinsic curiosity
about the vagaries of individual human behaviour but also
have a place in the different human studies. Psychologists,
psychiatrists, criminologists and anthropologists may base
some of their work on short biographies or case studies. For
the historian they are of particular significance. Firstly, the

course of a person's life represents a natural context which can, to some extent at least, be lifted from the vaster and more unmanageable contexts of history. Secondly, in contemplating the life of an individual, the historian can scrutinize—as it were in miniature—some of the processes, such as the setting of purposes, the clash of wills, or frustration by circumstances, which make up the stuff of history. Thirdly, by selecting for his study persons of central historical significance, Caesar, Luther or Lenin, he achieves a favourable point of view from which to understand an age or a set of historical circumstances. Certainly Dilthey does not consider history as simply the story of great men. Biography is only one of the historian's lines of approach.

We must now follow a characteristic turn in Dilthey's argument. While biographies form a basis for historical research they, in turn, depend on general historical knowledge. A person is the child of his age, acts in conjunction with other people, influences them and is affected by them. In studying him we must take into account the world he lived in. His biography thus widens out into historical narrative. There must, of course, be some limits to the painting of historical background and these are provided by the pattern of the person's life. A man may have been particularly influenced by certain features of his age, have participated in particular activities and affected particular spheres of life. These, but not others, have to be taken into account. For the life of a reformer, for example, the social conditions, but not the music of an age, may be relevant. But the difficulty of establishing a proper balance between the account of a person's life and the context in which he lived still remains in every biography. Only in the case of figures of central historical importance can this problem be adequately solved. In other cases there remains the danger of exaggerating the importance of a person to his age, or of leaving the biographical and general historical parts of the work only loosely connected.

In the mutual involvement of biography and history we encounter a problem which, in various forms, recurs in the human studies and, in fact, characterizes them. General knowledge about human nature and the various generalizations of psychology, sociology or political science are based on the understanding of individuals, yet these individuals can only be understood in terms of that general knowledge. History itself, which is concerned with individual phenomena, provides material for the systematic human studies and, at the same time, utilizes the generalizations of these studies to comprehend the historical course of events. None of the methods of the human studies has absolute epistemological priority but each depends on the others.

Dilthey's emphasis on the understanding of the individual, on autobiography and biography, illuminates his whole conception of history. He considers it the chief task of history to present us with a panorama of what human beings were like and how they acted. This task has vital importance because man knows himself not through introspection alone but through history. Only there do we glimpse the range of human potentialities as they have been realized in different places and ages.

This stress on the individual not only reveals Dilthey's conception of history but also something of his broad philosophical outlook, the moral and political implications of which are relevant in our age. There is no one 'meaning of life' but only the meaning which individuals have perceived in, or attributed to their own lives in terms of certain ideas and values. Each life has its own focal point, or points, around which it is more or less consistently organized and only in terms of these can it be understood. Any monolythic conception of history, any monolythic philosophy of life, stands, therefore, condemned. Dilthey sides quite clearly and decisively with those who want to allow individuals to shape their own destinies and rejects any authoritarian imposition of a uniform view of life.

TEXT

Pages 199-201. Part III. Autobiography
Autobiography is the highest and most instructive form in which the understanding of life confronts us. Here is the outward, phenomenal course of a life which forms the basis for

understanding what has produced it within a certain environment. The man who understands it is the same as the one who created it. A particular intimacy of understanding results from this. The person who seeks the connecting threads in the history of his life has already, from different points of view, created a coherence in that life which he is now putting into words. He has created it by experiencing values and realizing purposes in his life, making plans for it, seeing his past in terms of development and his future as the shaping of his life and of whatever he values most. He has, in his memory, singled out and accentuated the moments which he experienced as significant; others he has allowed to sink into forgetfulness. The future has corrected his illusions about the significance of certain moments. Thus, the first problem of grasping and presenting historical connections is already half solved by life. The units are formed by the conceptions of experience in which present and past events are held together by a common meaning. Among these experiences are those which have a special dignity both in themselves and for the course of his life; they have been preserved by memory and lifted out of the endless stream of what has happened and been forgotten. Constantly changing connections have been formed from different standpoints within life itself, so that the task of historical presentation is already half performed by life. Units, because they are experiences, have already taken shape; from an endless, countless, multiplicity, a selection of what is worth recording has been prepared. Between the parts we see a connection which neither is, nor is it intended to be, the simple likeness of the course of a life of so many years, but which, because understanding is involved, expresses what the individual knows about the continuity of his life.

Here we approach the root of all historical comprehension. Autobiography is merely the literary expression of a man's reflection on the course of his life. Such reflection, though it may be limited in extent, is frequently made by every individual. It is always present and expresses itself in ever new forms. It is present in the verses of Solon as well as in the reflections of the Stoic philosophers, in the meditations of the saints and in the philosophy of life of modern times. It, alone, makes historical insight possible. The power and breadth of our own lives and the energy with which we reflect on them are the foundation of historical vision. It alone enables us to give life back to the bloodless shadows of the past. Combined with an infinite desire to surrender to and lose one's self in the existence of others, it makes the great historian.

Pages 198-199. Part III. The Pattern of Life
I will now look at those autobiographies which are the most direct expressions of reflection on life. Augustine, Rousseau and Goethe, produced the typical forms in the history of autobiography. How do these writers grasp the continuity between the different parts of their lives? Augustine directs himself exclusively to the relationship of his life to God. His work is at one and the same time religious meditation, prayer and narrative. This leads up to the climax of his conversion and every previous event is only a milestone on the road to this consummation in which the purpose of providence with this particular man is fulfilled. Sensual enjoyment, philosophic delight, the rhetorician's pleasure in the splendour of speech, the circumstances of life, have no intrinsic value for him. In all these he feels the actual content strangely mixed with longing for that transcendental relationship; they are all transitory and only in his conversion does an eternal relationship, untainted by suffering, arise. Thus, to understand his life, we must relate its parts to the realization of an absolute value, an unconditional highest good. Looking back, we grasp the meaning of the earlier features of his life in terms of this relationship; we find not development but preparation for the turning away from all its transitory contents; As for Rousseau : — the way he related himself to his life in the Confessions can only be grasped in the same categories of meaning, values, significance and purpose. All France swarmed with rumours about his marriage, about his past. Misanthropic to the point of persecution mania and in dreadful loneliness he contemplated the incessant intrigues of his enemies against him. When he looked back in memory he saw himself driven from his calvinistically strict home, struggling upwards from

an obscure life of adventure to the active use of the greatness within him, soiled on the way by the dirt of the streets forced to put up with bad food of all descriptions, impotent in the face of the domination of the elegant world and of the leading intellects around him. But, whatever he had done and suffered and whatever was corrupt within him, he felt, and this was, after all, the ideal of his age, that he was a noble, generous soul who felt for humanity. This he wanted to show the world; he wanted to justify his spiritual existence by showing it exactly as it was. Here, too, the course of the outer events of a life has been interpreted. We have looked for connections which are not merely those of cause and effect. To name these we can only find such words as value, purpose, significance, meaning. If we look more closely we see that it is only through a special relation of these categories to each other that interpretation takes place. Rousseau wanted, above all, to justify his individual existence. This is a new conception, revealing infinite possibilities for giving value to life. From this point of view the relationship between the categories in terms of which he understood life is determined. And now for Goethe. *In Dichtung und Wahrheit* a man looks at his own existence from the standpoint of universal history. He sees himself in the context of the literary movement of his age. He has the calm proud consciousness of his position within it. So, to the old man looking back, every moment of his existence is doubly significant, both as an enjoyed fullness of life and as an effective force in the context of life. He feels in Leipzig, in Strasbourg, or in Frankfurt, that the present is always filled and determined by the past and that it stretches towards the shaping of the future—and thus he feels it to be a development. Here we can see more deeply into the relations of the categories as tools of understanding life. The significance of life lies in its shaping and its development; because of this the meaning of the parts of life is determined in a particular way; it is both the experienced intrinsic value of the moment and its effective power.

Every life has its own significance. This lies in a context of meaning in which every moment that can be remembered has an intrinsic value and, yet, in the context of memory, it also has a relation to the meaning of the whole. The significance of an individual existence is quite unique and so cannot be fathomed by knowledge; yet, in its way, like one of Leibniz's monads, it represents the historical universe.

Pages 246-248. Part III. The Scientific Nature of Biography
The task of all history is to grasp the systems of interactions. The historiographer penetrates more deeply into the structure of the historical world by sorting out and studying individual contexts. Religion, art, the state, political and religious organizations, form such contexts and permeate history. The most fundamental of these contexts is the course of an individual life in the environment by which it is affected and which it affects; it is present in the memory of an individual. Here we have the germinal cell of history, for here the specific historical categories arise. Because the sequence of a life is held together by the consciousness of identity, all the moments of that life have their foundation in the category of identity. The discrete is linked into continuity; by following the lines of memory from the small figure of childhood living for the moment, to the man who maintains his firm resolute inner life in the face of the world, we can relate the succession of influences and reactions to something which is shaping itself and which, thus, develops as something inwardly determined. The value of outer events which affect this self lies in the fact that they do so. The different states of this self and the influences at work on it have a meaning in their relation to the course of the life and to what is shaped within it.

Autobiography is the literary expression of the individual's reflection on his life. When this reflection is transferred to the understanding of another's existence it emerges in the form of a biography.

Every life can be described, the insignificant as well as the powerful, the everyday as well as the exceptional. Different points of view can produce the interest to do this. A family preserves its recollections. Criminology may record the life of a criminal, psychopathology that of an abnormal person. Everything human forms a document which conjures up one of the infinite potentialities of our existence. But the historical individual whose existence leaves a permanent mark, is worthy, in a higher sense, to live on in a biography which is a work of art. Among these, those whose actions have arisen from the depths of human life which are not easy to understand will draw the particular attention of the biographer. They allow us a deeper insight into human life and its individual forms.

How can one deny that biography is of outstanding significance for the understanding of the great context of the historical world? After all, it is the interaction between the depths of human nature and the universal context of broad historical life which has an effect at every point of history and this is the most fundamental connection between life itself and history.

Our problem becomes all the more urgent; is biography possible?

The course of a historical personality's life is a system of interactions in which the individual receives stimuli from the historical world, is moulded by them and, then, in his turn, affects the historical world. The stimuli originate in part of the world context which, in its turn, is shaped by the actions of the individual. The possibility of scientific biography lies in the fact that the individual does not face a limitless play of forces in the historical world; he lives in the sphere of the state, of religion, or of science—in other words, in a specific system of life or in a combination of them. It is the inner structure of this combination which attracts and forms the individual and determines the direction of his activities; historical achievements arise from the potentialities in the inner structure of a historical being.

Page 249 middle—251. Part III. Biography as a Work of Art

Biography has this advantage over autobiography; all the outer events of a life, right up to the time of death, can become the subject matter of understanding; the only limit is the amount of material preserved.

Biography can avail itself of statements about awareness of

what is meaningful as a basis for understanding. Some letters show what the individual considers valuable in a particular situation; others what he finds meaningful in the individual parts of his past. Connections form and lead to understanding —a talent expands, becomes aware of itself; circumstances, errors, passions may impede it, or a fortunate environment strengthen its creative power; it encounters external tasks which, for better or worse, lead it beyond itself, and so on. Yet there always remans the advantage that the course of a life preserves the relation between the outer and something inner, which is the meaning of that life; the testimonies themselves, like Goethe's confession, express this relationship. The spectator is already conscious of historical effects, their limits, and so on.

Letters reveal the writer's life at the time of writing. But they are influenced by the fact that they are directed to a recipient. They show relationships within life but every relationship is seen from one side only. Yet, if the meaning of a life, completed or even become part of history, can now be evaluated, this is only possible because, by interpreting documents, we can determine its connections with the past, the influence of its environment and the achievements of the future. These documents show the individual as a centre of forces which act on him and proceed from him. But the meaning of his life in the historical context can only be ascertained if we can establish a general pattern which can be separated from the individual person.

Biography as a work of art, therefore, cannot accomplish this task without turning to the history of the period.

But, with this, the point of view is changed. The interpretation of an individual life is limited because, being centred on himself, he must be made the focal point by his biographer. For biography to be a work of art a point of view must be found from which the general historical horizon can be seen; at the same time the individual must remain in the centre of a dynamic and meaningful system; no biography can perform this task with more than partial success. I must show, objectively, the meaningful context produced by varied forces which are determined by history and have a specific value;

the consciousness of infinity stretching out in every direction must always be present and yet the point of reference in the individual must be retained. From this it follows that biography as a work of art can only be applied to historical personalities, for only they have the power to become such a centre.

The difficulty of establishing what we may call the dual point of view of the biographer can never be wholly surmounted.

The importance of biography in historiography has increased extraordinarily. It was anticipated by the novel. Carlyle was, perhaps, the first to grasp its full significance, which lies in the fact that the greatest problem to arise since the development of the historical school up to the time of Ranke is the relationship between life in its manysidedness and historiography. This relationship is what history should preserve as a whole. All ultimate questions about the value of history find their answer in this—that, in it, man comes to know himself. It is not through introspection that we comprehend human nature. (This was Nietzsche's immense illusion. Therefore he could not grasp the significance of history). The more comprehensive task of history which thus arises was implicit in Hegel. We made further progress by studying the relatively unhistorical life of primitive peoples, for there we were confronted with the uniform repetition of lives identical in their content. This is like the natural foundation of all history. Quite a new kind of research was called forth by the most highly developed human personalities. Between these two lies the study of customs. Carlyle's biography, Jakob Burkhardt's grasping of an individual cultural whole from its foundations upwards, Macaulay's descriptions of customs, were the starting points. These are the foundations on which biography as a work of art has gained new meaning and new content.

Biography is limited by the fact that universal movements intersect in the individual life; if we are to understand them we must seek for new foundations outside the individual. It is not possible for biography to become scientific. *We must turn to new categories, shapes and forms of life which do not*

92

emerge from the individual life. The individual is only the crossing point for the cultural systems and organizations into which his existence is woven; how can they be understood through him?

Page 141-143. Part II. The Interdependence of Processes in Understanding

We have seen how the truths of the human studies rest on experience and understanding; but, on the other hand, understanding presupposes the use of the truths of the human studies. I will illustrate this by an example. Suppose we are trying to understand Bismarck. Our material consists of an extraordinary wealth of letters, documents, anecdotes and accounts about him. All this refers to his life. To understand what influenced this great statesman and what he achieved the historian must extend the range of this material. As long as the process of understanding goes on the collection of material has not been completed. To recognize that people, events and circumstances belong to this context involves the use of some generalizations. Therefore these also form the basis for the understanding of Bismarck. Such insights range from common human attributes to those of particular classes. From the point of view of the psychology of individuals the historian will place Bismarck among the men of action and trace in him the particular combination of characteristics common to them all. From another point of view he will recognize in the independence of his nature, in his habit of dominating and leading, and in his unbroken will, the characteristics of the Prussian landed aristocracy. As his long life occupies a specific place in the course of Prussian history another group of general statements must determine the features common to people of that age. The enormous pressure which the circumstances of his country exerted on political self-confidence naturally evoked the most varied reactions. To understand this demands general statements about the pressure which a situation exerts on a political whole and its parts and about their reaction. The degree of methodological certainty achieved by understanding depends on the development of the general truths on which the understanding of this relation is based. It now becomes clear that this great man of action, whose roots lay in Prussia and its monarchy, must have experienced the external pressure exerted on Prussia in a particular way. He, therefore, of necessity, judged the internal question of the constitution of the state mainly from the point of view of the power of the state. Because common factors like the state, religion, the law of the land, meet in him and because, as a historical personality, he was a force determined to a considerable degree and moved by these common factors, while, at the same time, affecting them, the historian needs a general knowledge of these factors. Put briefly, his understanding will only be ultimately perfected through its relationship with the essence of all the human studies. Every relationship which must be elaborated in presenting this historical personality reaches the highest achieveable certainty and clarity only when determined by scientific concepts about the individual spheres. The relation between these spheres is founded ultimately on a total conception of the historical world.

Thus, our example illuminates the double relation involved in understanding. Understanding presupposes experience and experience only becomes insight into life if understanding leads us from the narrowness and subjectivity of experience to the whole and the general. Moreover, the understanding of an individual personality to be complete demands systematic knowledge, while systematic knowledge is equally dependent on the vivid grasping of the individual. Knowledge of inorganic nature proceeds through a hierarchy of sciences in which the lower stratum is always independent of the one for which it lays the foundations; in the human studies everything from the process of understanding onwards is determined by the relationship of *mutual dependence*.

CHAPTER III

INDIVIDUAL LIFE AND ITS MEANING

EDITOR'S INTRODUCTION

The historian must tell a meaningful story and the meaning with which he imbues his account is already present in human life. How does it arise and how can we know it? Dilthey planned his work as a continuation of the Kantian Critiques, a Critique of Historical Reason, in fact. He therefore formulated a question analogous to those at the beginning of each of Kant's Critiques and asked; How is meaningful experience possible? Dilthey's epistemological position hinges on the answer to this question. In this chapter I have therefore, assembled passages which, together, constitute Dilthey's answer.

Awareness of meaning characterizes human life in general and provides the unifying framework of individual experiences. This meaning is not constituted by reference to something transcendental but by relations within life. We can grasp these by unbiased attention to the concrete reality of our lives. There is, to start with, the temporal structure of our lives. What we experience is not time by the clock, not the succession of tiny unconnected units of time. Every moment carries with it some awareness of the past and an anticipation of the future. What we call the present is always something with a temporal structure of its own and filled with some content of thought, feeling, or desire. Thus lived time has already a distinctive quality. Mental life has also some inherent structures through which different types of mental operations are linked together; sense impressions stir memories, memories awaken feelings, feelings arouse desires, desires may issue in actions. Acquired structures overlay the inherent ones.

When we talk about a person's love of music we are referring to moments of his life, to experiences and actions, which are singled out and linked to each other in some pattern. Thus, every experience contains a complex pattern. Take the example of listening to a piece of music. At any moment there must be awareness of the notes which have gone before and anticipation of those to come. There is enrichment of experience derived from previous hearings of the piece. There is an interlocking of sense experiences, thoughts, feelings, memories and, perhaps, desires. All this makes up the meaning of the experience.

We approach this meaning through what Dilthey calls the categories of life. By categories he means, by and large, the same as Kant did. They are the general forms of predications about life which, on the one hand, refer to what constitutes it as what it is and, on the other, provide the means of comprehending it. They are, though, and here Dilthey diverges from Kant, derived from experience itself and cannot, therefore, be wholly formalized, nor exhaustively listed.

At times Dilthey talks of meaning as one of the categories, namely the one through which the pattern of the past is reconstituted in memory. He then places this category of the past beside 'value' as the category of the present and 'purpose' as the category of the future and assumes that each of these categories, from a different point of view, organizes the whole of experience. I believe that it is a more consistent interpretation of Dilthey's final view to consider meaning as the master category which characterizes all human life and all the other categories as different ways in which this meaning is constituted.

To illustrate this point and to explain some of the terms which Dilthey uses I shall list some of these categories.

Value–something is meaningful insofar as it is valued, that is, appreciated, loved, hated, resented, by a person.

Purpose–something is meaningful insofar as it forms a person's goal or serves as a means to that goal.

Part and Whole–something is meaningful insofar as it is part of a pattern or a link in a chain. A whole, in turn, is meaningful in terms of the meaning of the parts.

Inner and Outer–something is meaningful insofar as it is the outer expression of some inner process, a thought, a feeling, or an act of will.

Formation–something is meaningful insofar as it embodies a shape, pattern or configuration.

Development–a course of events is meaningful insofar as the successive changes are cumulatively influenced by the previous ones.

Power–a situation is meaningful insofar as we affect it by our decisions and actions, or insofar as we are affected by forces outside us. In the studies of man this category is the equivalent of the category of causality, but the latter is, psychologically speaking a derivation from, or abstraction of, the category of power.

Human experiences and, indeed, human lives, have concrete meaning in terms of these categories and, by means of them, this meaning can be recaptured. But, and here Dilthey develops further a thought we have already encountered, individuals cannot be understood in isolation. We have to take into account what human beings have in common, that is, at its most general, human nature and, more specifically, the shared characteristics of nations, classes, or other groups. From this point of view the infinite variety of human nature can be explained in terms of the different degrees to which individuals possess these common characteristics. This quantitative approach, combined with attention to environmental influences, can make an important contribution to the understanding of individuals.

TEXT

Pages 71-74. Part I. The Delimitation of the Human Studies (third study)

The only complete, self-contained and clearly defined happening encountered everywhere in history and in every concept that occurs in the human studies, is the course of a life. This forms a context circumscribed by birth and death. It is perceived externally in the continuing existence of the person during the span of his life. This continuity is unbroken. But, independent of this, there exist experienceable connections which link the parts of the course of a life from birth to death. A decision will produce actions which extend over many years; in spite of long interruptions by occurrences of quite a different kind that decision will influence actions without any new decision to the effect being made. Work on a chain of ideas can be separated by long stretches of time and yet the task which is now resumed was set at a time long past. A plan of life can persist without being re-examined and link the most varied decisions, actions, resistance, wishes and hopes. In brief, there are connections quite independent of the temporal sequence and the direct causal relations in it, which join the parts of a life into a whole. Thus, the unity of a life is actually experienced and is securely based on such experience.

The course of life is something temporal; that is what the expression 'course' means. Time is not just a line consisting of parts of equal value, a system of relations, of succession, simultaneity and continuity. If we think of time apart from what fills it, its parts are of equal value. Even the smallest part of this continuum is linear, a succession of parts; nowhere, even in the smallest part, is there anything which 'is'. Concrete time consists rather of the uninterrupted progress of the present, what was present constantly becoming the past and the future becoming the present. The present is the filling of a moment of time with reality; this is experience, in contrast to the memory of it, or to the wishes, hopes, expectations and fears about something which may be experienced in the future. This filling up with reality is what persists continuously and always as time progresses, though the content of experience is constantly changing. This progressive filling up with reality along the line of time characteristic of the present, in contrast to ideas of what has been experienced and may yet be experienced, this constant sinking backwards of the present into the past and the becoming present of that which a moment ago we still expected, wanted, or feared, of that which was only in the region of ideas—this is the character of real time. Thus, it follows that we always live in the present and our lives are constantly corruptible. This progressive filling of the moments of time with reality also means that the present within the sequence of events—where its continuity is not broken by sleep or similar states—follows on without breach or gap and is always there. Only in the present is there fullness of time and, therefore, fullness of life. The ship of our life is, as it were, carried along on an everflowing river and the present is always where we live, suffer, strive and remember; in brief, where we experience the fullness of our reality. But we are constantly sailing with the stream and the moment the future becomes the present it sinks into the past. The difference between experience—including the experiences of remembering, of expecting a future and willing its realization—and its content, that is, ideas of something past or future, is familiar. For, the relationship between present, past and future is characteristic of our lives. But, as the present never persists and, as even the smallest part of the continuous progression of time contains the present and the memory of what has just been present, it follows that the present as such can never be experienced. To this we must add that the continuity between what we remember and the present, the continued existence of a qualitatively determined reality, and the continued effectiveness of the past as a power in the present, give to what is remembered a peculiar characteristic of 'being present'. This is the involving of the past in our actual experience. The smallest unit which we can describe as an experience is whatever forms a meaningful unit in the course of a life. In addition, linguistic usage also calls an experience any more comprehensive ideal unit of parts of a life which has a meaning for that life; it uses this concept even when the elements are separated by interrupting events.[1]

Thus we come face to face with the category of meaning. The relation contained in it defines and clarifies the conception we have of our lives; it is also the point of view from which we grasp and describe the coexistence and sequence of lives in history, emphasizing what is significant and meaningful and thus shaping every event; it is, quite generally, the

[1] A performance of 'The Ring', for example, can be regarded as *one* experience even if we have seen the parts on successive nights.

category which is peculiar to life and to the historical world; indeed, it is inherent in life because it is the particular relationship which exists between its parts; all life contains this relationship which is essential for describing it.

I can see the particular connections of my life in time only insofar as I can recollect its course. A long series of events combines actively in my memory; not one of them can be reproduced in isolation. As selection has already taken place in my memory individual experiences were either relevant for the understanding of my life just when they occurred or remained so in the evaluation of a later time, or became so, while I still remembered them, from a new conception of my life; this relevance forms the principle of selection and, now that I think back, from all that I can still recall, only what is meaningful in the light of my present view of it receives a place in the context of my life. Hence, my present conception of life determines how I see every significant part of it today. From this it receives its relation to other significant parts; it belongs to a context determined by the relation between the significant moments of life and my present interpretation of them. These meaning relationships constitute my present experience and permeate it. If a person who means something to me visits me this experience receives its richness from what was significant in former meetings; the older experiences are merged into a stronger unity which arises from their reference to the present. I can, then, feel as if I had never been separated from this person; so inward and peculiar is this relationship. I have repeatedly visited a certain art gallery; from what was meaningful to me in the past there now develops the whole fullness of the present artistic experience, however much time may separate today's visit from the last.

Autobiography is the expression of all this. It is an interpretation of life in its mysterious combination of chance, destiny and character. Wherever we look our minds struggle to come to terms with life. We suffer from our destinies and our natures which force us to acceptance through understanding. The past lures us mysteriously on to try to understand the web of meaning of its elements. Yet interpretation remains unsatisfactory. We never master what we call chance the wonderful and dreadful that become significant for our lives always seem to enter through the door of chance.

Pages 24-25. Part I. Delimitation of Objective Apprehension

Ideas, judgements, feelings, desires and acts of will are interwoven everywhere in the system of the mind; thus we know about mental life empirically. A harmonious combination of sounds evokes a feeling of approval; then a visual impression intrudes into this calm, aesthetic enjoyment and reproduces memories; thus a desire arises; on the grounds of a judgement this is suppressed through fear of the consequences of satisfying it;[1] and so the empirical facts of mental life show that all types of mental processes are interwoven; and the uniformities which we find existing in this genetic context of mental events refer to the co-operation of the manifold factors interwoven in this way. So the reproduction of our ideas is as much conditioned by the interest and attention with which impressions have been received and reproduced as by the composition of the ideas and the number of times they have recurred.

This manifold interweaving of different factors into the genetic context of mental processes is permeated by various kinds of inner relations; each of these is characterized by the fact that it links the experiences belonging to it into a system. The relations within such a system form one of the main parts of the fundamental pattern which is, as it were, the anatomical structure of the firmly and regularly developed mental system. One of these inner relations exists between perceptions, remembered ideas, judgements and combinations of judgements culminating in the system of knowledge. Whatever else may be contained in these experiences each of them shows a certain kind of consciousness of content which we describe as objective apprehension. The system of these ex-

[1] A piece of music, for example, may evoke the memory of a girl I used to know. I would like to see her again but decide against it because she is married to a jealous husband.

periences is characterized by the uniform way in which structural unity is produced by acts of this kind.[1]

Pages 139-140. Part II. How Representation is Based on Experience

What happens when an experience becomes the object of my reflection? I lie awake at night worrying about the possibility of completing in my old age works I have already begun; I consider what is still to be done. My awareness of all this forms a structured whole based on objective comprehension; from this arises an attitude of care and sorrow about the facts thus objectively grasped and of determination to get beyond it. All this is before me as a connected whole. I bring this situation to discriminating consciousness. I abstract the structural connections and isolate them. All that I thus abstract is contained in the experience itself and is only being illuminated. Now my comprehension of the experience itself is carried by elements contained within it on to experiences which, in the course of my life, though separated by long stretches of time, were structurally connected with them. I know about my works, having previously reviewed them; linked to them in the far distant past are the processes by which they originated. Another element leads into the future; work in progress will yet demand incalculable labour; I worry about it; I prepare myself inwardly for the task. All this 'about' 'from' and 'towards' all these relations to what has been lived and remembered or still lies in the future carries me along backwards and forwards. Because living through an experience calls for ever new links, we are carried along in this way. Interest, originating in the emotive power of the experience, may also play its part. It is a being carried along, not a volition, least of all an abstract will to knowledge to which it has been attributed since Schleiermacher's Dialectic. In the sequence which then arises the past, as well as the possible future, is transcendent to the moment filled with experience. But both past and future elements are related to the experience in a sequence which, through these relation-

[1] This is merely the description of one type of mental process—the making of factual judgements.

ships, is welded into a whole. Because remembering involves recognition everything past is structurally related to a former experience by being a reproduction of it. Future possibilities are also linked to the sequence because of the range of potentialities mapped out by it. Thus, in this process, there arises a view of the continuity of mental life in time which constitutes the course of a life. In this every single experience is related to the whole. This connectedness of life is not a sum or quintessence of successive moments but a unity constituted by relationships which link all the parts. From the present we run through a series of memories back to the point where our small malleable and unformed self is lost in the twilight and penetrate forward from the present to possibilities which are grounded in it but at the same time assume vague and vast dimensions.

Thus there arises a conclusion important for the mutual relations of the studies concerned with man. The elements, regularities and relations which constitute the conception of the course of a life are all contained in it. The knowledge of the course of one's life is as real as experience itself.

Pages 201-202. Part III. Autobiography
What is it, then, which, in the contemplation on one's life links the parts into a whole and thus makes it comprehensible? It is the fact that understanding involves, in addition to the general categories of thought, those of value, purpose and meaning. Comprehensive concepts like the shaping and development of human life are subsumed under these. The differences between these categories are, in the first resort, determined by the point of view from which the course of a life is reviewed.

Looking back at the past in memory we see, in terms of the category of meaning, how the parts of a life are linked together. In the present we feel the positive or negative value of the realities which fill it and, as we look towards the future, the category of purpose arises. We see life as the achieving of over-riding purposes to which all individual purposes are subordinated, that is, as the realizing of a supreme good.

None of these categories can be subordinated to the other as each of them makes the whole of life accessible to the understanding from a different point of view. They are incommensurable.

And yet, there is a distinction in the way they are related to the understanding of a life. The intrinsic values experienced in, and only in, the living present are directly accessible to experience but are not connected with each other.[1] Each of them arises in the relation of a subject to an object present to him at the time. By contrast, when we set ourselves a purpose we relate ourselves to the idea of an object which is to be achieved. Thus the intrinsic values of the experienced present stand, unconnected, beside each other; they can only be compared with each other and evaluated. Anything else described as valuable refers only to relationships to intrinsic values. If we ascribe an objective value to an object this only means that we can have some value experience or other when it exists. If we ascribe an instrumental value to it we describe it as capable of bringing about something valuable later. All these are purely logical relationships into which a value, experienced in the present, can enter. Life, from the point of view of value, thus appears as an infinite multiplicity of positive and negative existential values. It is like a chaos of chords and discords. Each is a structure of notes which fills a present but has no musical relation to the others. The category of purpose, or of good, which considers life as directed towards the future, presupposes that of value. The connectedness of life cannot be established from this category either, for the relations of purposes to each other are only those of possibility, choice and subordination. Only the category of meaning goes beyond mere co-existence or subordination of the parts of life.[2] As history is memory and as the category of meaning belongs to memory, this is the category which belongs most intimately to historical thinking. We must now enlarge on its gradual development.

[1] For instance, enjoyment of a cigar and pleasure in a landscape.
[2] If we regard Judaism merely as a preparation for Christianity, we should be thinking in terms of purpose and, therefore, of subordination. Dilthey rejects such treatment of history.

Pages 232-236. Part III. Meaning

A new aspect of life, conditioned by time but, being something new, transcending it, now becomes apparent. The special character of life is understood by means of categories which do not apply to our knowledge of physical reality. Here, too, the decisive point is that these categories are not applied *a priori* to life as something strange but that they are part of it. The attitude expressed abstractly in them is the exclusive point of departure for the understanding of life. For life is only to be found in the special relation between a whole and its parts; and, if we abstract these relations as categories, we find that the number of these cannot be determined and their relations to each other cannot be reduced to a logical formula. Meaning, value, purpose, development, ideal, are such categories. But they all depend on the fact that the connectedness of a life can only be understood through the meaning the individual parts have for understanding the whole and that every part of the life of mankind can only be understood in the same way. Meaning is the comprehensive category through which life becomes comprehensible.

The objects of the physical world are as changeable as self-conscious life; but only in the latter does the present embrace ideas of the past in memory and of the future in imagination (which traces its possibilities) and activity (which sets purposes among these possibilities). Thus the present is filled with the past and carries the future within itself. This is the meaning of the word 'development' in the human studies. It does not mean that we can apply to the life of the individual, of the nation, or of mankind, the concept of a purpose to be realized; this would be an external way of looking at the subject and could be rejected.[1] With this concept of development goes that of formation.[2] Formation is a general characteristic of life. If we look more deeply into life we find formation even in the poorest souls. We see it most clearly in great men

---

[1] In other words development means continuity of change based on the cumulative effect of the past. It does not mean progress, i.e. advance towards the realization of a goal.

[2] Formation, or an equivalent, like configuration, does not carry the full meaning of the German word *Gestaltung*. It has to be understood as defined in the text.

with a historical destiny; but no life is so poor that formation does not occur in it. Wherever structure and, based on it, acquired patterns of mental life, form a permanent basis preserved through change and decay, the course of a life in time becomes formation. Yet this concept can only occur because we comprehend life in terms of the category of meaning.

The category of meaning designates the relation, rooted in life itself, of parts to the whole. This connection is only present in memory through which we can survey our past. There meaning asserts itself as the way of comprehending life. We grasp the meaning of a moment of the past. It is significant for the individual because, in it, an action or outer event committed him for the future or a plan for the conduct of his life was made or carried forward to realization; it is significant for the community because an individual intervened in its life, affecting the formation of mankind by his own essential nature. In all these and other cases the single moment derives its meaning from its connection with the whole, from the relation between future and past, between the individual and mankind. But what does this particular relation of part to whole within life consist of?

It is a relation which is never complete. One would have to wait for the end of a life and, in the hour of death, survey the whole to ascertain the relation between the whole and its parts. One would have to wait for the end of history to have all the material necessary to determine its meaning. On the other hand the whole is only there for us when it becomes comprehensible through its parts. Understanding is for ever suspended between these two lines of approach. Our conception of the meaning of a life is constantly changing. Every plan for a life expresses a conception of the meaning of life. The purpose we set for the future conditions how we determine the meaning of the past. The actual pattern of life is judged in terms of the meaning we give to what we remember.

Just as words have meaning through which they designate something, or sentences a significance which we can construe, so can the pattern of life be construed from the determined—undetermined meaning of its parts.

Meaning is the special relation which the parts have to the whole within a life. We recognise this meaning as we do that of words in a sentence, through memory and the potentialities of the future. The nature of the meaning relations lies in the pattern of a life formed in time by the interaction between a living structure and its environment.

What is it, then, which, in the contemplation of one's life, constitutes the pattern which links the parts into a whole and makes the life comprehensible? An experience is a unit made up of parts linked by a common meaning. The narrator achieves his effect by emphasizing the significant elements of a course of events. The historian describes certain human beings as significant and certain turning points in life as meaningful; he recognizes the significance of a work or a man by its special effect on the common destiny. The parts of a life have a certain meaning for the whole; put briefly, the category of meaning has obviously a particularly close *connection with understanding*; this we must now try to comprehend.

Every expression of life has a meaning insofar as it is a sign which expresses something that is part of life. Life does not mean anything other than itself. There is nothing in it which points to a meaning beyond it.

If we single out something in it by means of concepts this serves above all to describe the unique quality of life. These general concepts serve, therefore, to express an understanding of life. Here there is only a loose progression from the presupposition to what follows from it; what is new does not follow formally from the presupposition; it is rather that understanding passes from something already grasped to something new which can be understood through it. The inner relationship lies in the possibility of reproduction and empathy.[1] This is the general method to be used as soon as understanding leaves the sphere of words and their meaning and seeks not the meaning of signs but the much deeper

[1] For instance, capitalism does not arise inevitably and logically from Protestantism. Only by thinking himself into the attitude of Protestant sects could Max Weber understand how it promoted capitalist tendencies.

meaning of expressions of life. Fichte had the first inkling of this method. Life is like a melody the notes of which are not the expression of hidden realities within. Just as the notes of a melody express nothing but the melody so life expresses only itself.

The simplest case in which meaning occurs is the understanding of a sentence. Each word has a meaning and, by joining them, the meaning of the sentence is deduced. Here understanding of the sentence results from the meaning of the individual words. But there is an interaction between the whole and the parts through which ambiguities of meaning are eliminated and the meaning of the individual words determined.

The same relation holds between the parts and the whole of a life and here, too, the understanding of the whole, the significance of life (arises) from the meaning[1] . . .

This relation of meaning and significance holds, therefore, for the course of a life; individual events in the external world which form it, have, like the words in a sentence, a relation to something which they mean. Through this every experience is significantly connected up in terms of a whole. And just as the words of a sentence are joined to give it meaning, so experiences are connected to give us the meaning of a life. It is the same with history.

Thus the concept of meaning arises, first of all, in relation to the process of understanding. It contains the relation of something outward, something given to the senses, to something inward, of which it is the expression. But this relation is essentially different from the grammatical one. The expression of mental content in the parts of life is different from the expression of meaning by a word.

Hence such words as meaning, comprehension, significance (of a life or of history) are only pointers to the relation between events and an inner connection, contained in understanding and required by it.

We are looking for the kind of connection which is inherent in life itself; and we are looking for it in the individual events. In each of these which contributes to the context,

[1] The sentence is incomplete in Dilthey's text.

something of the meaning of life must be contained, otherwise it could not arise from their interconnection. The working model of the natural sciences is constituted by the concepts of a causal order in the physical world and their particular methodology consists of the procedures for discovering it; in an analogous way the categories of life, their relations to each other, the working model they constitute, and the methods used to grasp them, become accessible to us. But, in the one we are dealing with abstract connections, which, in their essence, are logically transparent. In the other we aim at understanding the connectedness of life itself which can never become wholly accessible to the understanding.

Our understanding of life is only a constant approximation; that life reveals quite different sides to us according to the point of view from which we consider its course in time, is due to the nature of both understanding and life. . . . .

Only in the relation of the meaning of the events of life to the understanding and significance of the whole do connections found in life receive adequate representation. Only here is co-existence or subordination transcended. Thus the categories of value and purpose which are individual aspects of the understanding of life become part of the comprehensive context of this form of understanding.

Pages 202-204. Part III. Supplement of 3. The Pattern of Life

In connection with the categories of doing and suffering there arises the category of power. Doing and suffering are, as we saw, the foundations of the principle of causality in the natural sciences. The principle in its strict form is developed in mechanics. In the natural sciences power is a hypothetical concept. Where its validity is assumed it is determined by the principle of causality. In the human studies power is the expression, in the form of a category, of something that can be experienced. It originates when we turn towards the future, which happens in different ways; in dreams of future happiness, in the play of the imagination with possibilities, in hesitation and in fear . . . But now let us gather together this idle expansion of our existence and concentrate on one point;

surrounded by various possibilities we decided to realize one of them. The idea of a purpose which now emerges contains something new which is to be brought into the circle of reality; here we have, quite independent of any theory about the will, a bracing up (which the psychologist might interpret physiologically), a purposefulness, the emergence of an intention to realize something, the selection and definition of a special goal, the choice of means for achieving it, as well as the achievement itself. The continuous process of life which produces all this we call power, a concept which is decisive for the human studies; however far they extend we are dealing with a coherent whole which, throughout, contains existing states of affairs; but, insofar as history strives to understand and express changes, it must operate with concepts which express energy, tendencies and regroupings of historical forces. The more historical concepts assume this character the better will they express the nature of their subject matter. What gives the fixing of an object in a concept its timeless validity is inherent only in its logical form. Therefore, it is necessary to form concepts which express the freedom of life and history. Hobbes says frequently that life is constant movement. Leibniz and Wolf say that happiness, for both the individual and the community, lies in the consciousness of progress.

All these categories of life and history are forms if not of empirical statements then of statements developed from them by additional thought processes, which become generally applicable in the human studies. They originate in experience itself. They are not super-added types of formation; the structural forms of life in its temporal course are expressed in them because of the formal operations founded on the unity of consciousness. What, then, is the subject matter of these categories? It is the course of a life which takes place in a human body and which, as a self, with its intentions and their frustration by pressure from the outside world, is distinguished from what is outside, impossible to experience and strange. But it is further determined by the predications already explained; and, thus, all our statements are already within the sphere of experience insofar as they are about the course of a life and so (in accordance with the nature of statements) express predicates about it, starting with predications about one special context. They achieve universality through having, as their background, the objective mind, and, as their constant counterpart, insight into other people. . . . .

The grasping and interpretation of one's own life takes place in a long series of stages; the most complete presentation is the autobiography. Here the self grasps the course of its own life in such a way as to bring to consciousness the basis of human life, namely the historical relations in which it is interwoven. The autobiography can, ultimately, widen out into a historical portrait; this is limited, but also made meaningful by being based on experience, through which the self and its relation to the world are comprehended. The reflection of a person about himself remains the point of orientation and foundation.

Pages 212-213. Part III. The Higher Forms of Understanding
The subject matter of understanding is always something individual. Understanding in its higher forms draws its conclusions about the pattern within a work, a person, or a situation from what is given in the book or person and combined by induction. But analysis and understanding of our own experience show that the individual is an intrinsic value in the mind-affected world; indeed, it is the only intrinsic value we can ascertain beyond doubt. Thus we are concerned with the individual as not merely an example of man in general but as himself. Quite independent of the practical interest which constantly forces us to reckon with other people, this concern, be it noble or wicked, vulgar or foolish, occupies a considerable place in our lives. The secret of personality lures us on to new attempts at deeper understanding for its own sake. And, in such understanding, the realm of individuals, embracing men and their creations, opens up. The peculiar contribution of understanding in the human studies lies in this; the objective mind and the power of the individual together determine the mind-affected world. History rests on the understanding of these two.

But we understand individuals by virtue of their kinship

with each other, by the features they have in common. This process presupposes a connection between what is common to man and what differentiates individuals. On the basis of this connection a variety of mental existences unfolds and through it we constantly accomplish the practical task of living through, as it were, in our minds, the unfolding of individuality. The material for the accomplishment of this task is formed by the facts combined by induction. Each fact has an individual character and is grasped as such; it therefore contains something which makes the comprehension of the individual features of the whole in its individuality, possible. But the presupposition on which this procedure is based assumes more and more developed forms as we become absorbed in the particular and the comparison of it with other things; thus the business of understanding takes us into ever greater depths of the mind-affected world. Just as the objective mind contains a structural order of types so does mankind and this leads from the regularity and structure of general human nature to the types through which understanding grasps individuals. If we assume that these are not distinguished qualitatively but, as it were, through emphasis on particular elements—however one may express this psychologically—then this represents the inner principle of the rise of individuality. And, if it were possible, in the act of understanding, to grasp the changes brought about by circumstances in the life and state of the mind, as the outer principle of the rise of individuality, and the varied emphasis on the structural elements as the inner principle, then the understanding of human beings and of poetic and literary works would be a way of approach to the greatest mystery of life. And this, in fact, is the case.[1]

[1] To illustrate : One of a man's characteristics is his intelligence. This he has in common with others but he is individually characterized by its degree and its relation to other qualities (the inner principle) as well as by the way in which circumstances have made him train and apply it (the outer).

CHAPTER IV

THE UNDERSTANDING OF OTHERS AND THE OBJECTIVE MIND

In the foregoing chapters we have seen Dilthey's insistence on three ideas which all point in the same direction. Firstly, that the self-awareness of the individual, his experience of the processes in his own mind and his personal sense of life form the basis for his understanding of the human world. Secondly, that the understanding of individual lives is fundamental for the understanding of society and history. Thirdly, that the study of the patterns which constitute the course of individual lives provides the evidence for the systematic human studies. It would, however, be a complete misunderstanding to consider Dilthey's epistemological position simply in terms of intuition, introspection, psychological finesse and the grasping of the unique. We have already encountered, particularly at the end of the two previous chapters, passages which place his theory on a much broader basis and counterbalance the above points. In the present chapter he underlines further the fact that the understanding of others helps us to understand ourselves, that individuals can only be understood in terms of the human, social and historical contexts in which they stand and that historical knowledge itself, that is, knowledge of successions of individual events, is made possible only by recourse to the findings of the systematic human studies.

At the beginning of this chapter Dilthey resumes his discussion of the ways in which we understand other people. First of all he takes up the study of expressions, which we have already encountered in the first chapter, introduces some further distinctions and considers the evidential value of different forms of expressions. There is, firstly, the class of what I shall call, for the sake of brevity, factual statements, including, for instance, all the assertions of science. These can carry precise and easily communicable meaning but, for the student of human nature, they have the disadvantage that they tell us little about the person who asserts them. There are, secondly, actions in which the intentions of the agents become transparent. These give us important but, as Dilthey maintains, one-sided information. Because actions arise from the challenge of particular circumstances only one of the agent's varied potentialities becomes visible in them. (Dilthey thereby rejects the position taken up by some thinkers, Sartre among them, that man is what he does.) Thirdly, there are what have been called the emotive expressions, the tear in the eye, the shout of joy, the lyrical effusion. These can reveal depths of the human mind but, in practical life, they can, of course, be untruthful and deceptive. Only in genuine works of art and literature do emotive expressions give us reliable insights into human nature, for it is the purpose of art to communicate meaning without any ulterior motive.

But—and here we have arrived at the complementary part of Dilthey's theory—understanding of all these different forms of expression presupposes the existence of a sphere which he describes variously as 'the objective mind', 'the objectifications of life', and 'the mind-affected world'. It is, roughly speaking, what social anthropologists have called the culture pattern and embraces social organization, beliefs, traditions, institutions, languages, religions and philosophies; in fact, everything human beings have created and in which they have embodied their thoughts, feelings and intentions.

Obviously we can only understand a scientific statement if we know the language in which it is made and possibly something about that science. We only understand what the intentions of a craftsman are when we know something about the way that craft is practised at that particular time and place. Even expressions of joy or grief can only be appreciated in terms of prevailing conventions. (The Homeric heroes freely gave way to tears but not so the heroes of Jane Austen.) Needless to say, works of art and literature can only be appreciated in terms of the rules, conventions and traditions within which the artist worked.

The nature of an individual person or event is determined by its place in and relation to the objective mind, that is, the objective structure which life—in the sense defined above—has assumed. This point will be further developed—with special reference to nations, ages and cultural systems and the place of individuals in them—in the next chapter.

The objective mind is not a metaphysical assumption but the succinct name for a range of empirical facts which we can understand because the human mind (not just the human intellect) has entered into them. To underline that nothing mysterious is implied let me give an illustration. A book is part of the objective mind. This means that it contains not only sheets of paper with black lines on them but human thought which we can recapture from these marks. This we do by reading them.

To understand the individual structures which constitute the objective mind we proceed in a way which is analogous to that through which we understand individual persons. We interpret the inner meaning of outer manifestations, relate part to whole, and, above all, try to grasp the focal point which gives them their unity. In other words, we try to comprehend the theme of a poem, the purpose of an organization or institution, the dominant beliefs of an age.

To complete the theoretical foundations of historical knowledge we must take one further step. We must show that the human world is a dynamic and not a static system. Dilthey discusses this point in terms of a concept which we must now explain. This is the 'Wirkungszusammenhang', which I have translated as 'system of interactions'. Throughout his work Dilthey is concerned with the totality of the human world, which he calls the 'social historical world', or, simply 'life'. Seen from the point of view of its basic structures and enduring manifestations he calls it objective mind, or the mind-affected world but, from the point of view of the unfolding patterns of human actions and their consequences, he calls it the 'system of interactions', (which, of course, contains sub-systems). This concept is linked to the category of power and is the equivalent in the human world of the causal order of nature. Because human actions—in contrast to natural events —are meaningful, purposive and free, the system of inter-actions is different from the order of nature because it is teleological and creative. It is in terms of this system of inter-actions that is, in terms of human striving, its success or frustration through circumstances, that the pageant of history must be understood.

TEXT

Page 220. Part III. Musical Understanding
Neither in its temporal flow nor in the depth of its content is the self fully accessible to us in experience. For the small area of conscious life rises like an island from inaccessible depths. But expression lifts something from out of these depths;[1] it is creative. And thus, in the process of understanding, life itself becomes accessible as a reproduction of creative activity. It is true we may have only a work of art before us and this, to go on existing, must be located in space; in notes, in letters, on a gramophone or, originally, in a memory; but what is thus fixed is the ideal representation of a course of events.

Pages 205-210. Part III. The Understanding of Others and their Expressions of Life
Understanding and interpretation is the method used through-out the human studies and all functions unite in it. It con-tains all the truths of the human studies. Everywhere under-standing opens up a world.

On the basis of experience and self-understanding and the constant interaction between them, understanding of other people and their expressions of life is developed. Here, too, it is not a matter of logical construction or psychological analysis but of an epistemological analysis. We must now

---

[1] Here we have a conception of unconscious mind not unlike that of Freud. Indeed, Freud's theories which, as is often forgotten, concentrate largely on certain aspects of the human mind can, by and large, be fitted into the theoretical framework of Dilthey's conception of man.

establish what understanding can contribute to historical knowledge.

What is given are always expressions of life; occurring in the world of the senses they are always expressions of a mind which they help us to understand. I include here not only expressions of life which mean or signify something but also those which, without intending to signify anything make the mind of which they are expressions comprehensible to us. The kind and amount of understanding is different according to the classes of expressions of life.

The first of these classes is formed by concepts, judgements and larger thought structures. As constituent parts of science, separated from the experience in which they occurred, they have a common fundamental character in their conformity to logical norms. They retain their identity, therefore, independently of the position in which they occur in the context of thought. Judgement asserts the validity of a thought content independently of the varied situations in which it occurs, the difference of time and of people involved. This is the meaning of the law of identity. Thus the judgement is the same for the man who makes it and the one who undestands it; it passes, as if transported, from the speaker into the possession of the one who understands it. This determines the kind of understanding for all logically perfect thought content which remains identical in every context and thus understanding is more complete here than in relation to any other expression of life. At the same time it does not express anything about its relations to the obscure and abundant life of the mind to the man who understands it. There is no hint of the peculiarities of the life from which it arose and it follows from its nature that it does not require us to go back to its psychological context.

Actions form another class of expressions of life. An action does not arise from the intention to communicate; however, because of the relation in which it stands to a purpose, the latter is contained in it. The relation of the action to the mind which it thus expresses is regular and so we can make assumptions about it. But it is certainly necessary to distinguish the state of mind conditioned by the circumstances which produces the action it expresses, from the context in life on which this state is based. Action, through the power of a decisive motive, steps from the plenitude of life into one-sidedness. However much it may have been considered it expresses only a part of our nature. It annihilates potentialities which lie in that nature. So action, too separates itself from the background of the content of life; and, unless accompanied by an explanation of how circumstances, purpose, means and context of life are linked together in it, it allows no comprehensive determination of the inner life from which it arose.[1]

It is quite different with emotive expressions (Erlebnisausdruck). A special relation exists between them, the life from which they arise and the understanding which they produce. For expressions can contain more of the psychological context than any introspection can discover. They lift it from depths which consciousness does not illuminate. But it is part of the nature of expressions that the relations between them and the mind which is expressed in them can provide only a limited basis for understanding. They are not subject to the judgement of true or false, but to that of truthful or untruthful. For dissimulation, lie, or deception can break the relation between expression and the mental content which is expressed.

Here an important distinction asserts itself and is the source of the highest significance to which expression can rise in the human studies. What springs from the life of the day is subject to the power of its interests. The interpretation of what is transitory is also determined by the moment. It is terrible that in the struggle of practical interests every expression can be deceptive and its interpretation changed with the change in our situation. But, in great works, because some content of the mind separates itself from its creator, the poet, artist, or writer, we enter a sphere in which deception ends. No truly great work of art can, according to the conditions

---

[1] Some thinkers, Sartre, for example, maintain that man's actions define what he is. In contrast, Dilthey believed that the potentialities of a man, even though circumstances prevent them from being realized, are relevant for understanding him.

which hold good and are to be developed later, wish to give the illusion of a mental content foreign to its author; indeed, it does not want to say anything about its author. Truthful in itself it stands—fixed, visible, permanent; and, because of this, a skilled and certain understanding of it is possible. Thus there arises in the confines between science and action a circle in which life discloses itself at a depth inaccessible to observation, reflection and theory.

Understanding arises, first of all, from the interests of practical life where people are dependent on communicating with each other. They must make themselves mutually understood. The one must know what the other wants. Thus, first of all, the elementary forms of understanding arise. They are like letters of the alphabet which, joined together, make higher forms of understanding possible. By such an elementary form I mean the interpretation of a single expression of life. Logically it can be represented as an argument from analogy. The regular relation between the expression and what is expressed forms the link in the argument. In each of the classes listed individual expressions can be interpreted in this way. A series of letters combined into words which form a sentence is the expression of an assertion. A facial expression signifies pleasure or pain. The elementary acts of which continuous activities are composed, such as the picking up of an object, the dropping of a hammer, the cutting of wood with a saw, indicate the presence of certain purposes. In this elementary understanding we do not go back to the whole context of life which forms the permanent subject of the expressions of life. We are also not conscious of any deduction from which this understanding could have arisen.

The fundamental relationship on which the process of elementary understanding rests, is that of the expression to what it expresses. Elementary understanding is not an inference from an effect to a cause. Nor must we, with greater caution, grasp it as a procedure which goes back from the given reality to some part of the context of life which made the effect possible. Certainly the latter relation is contained in the circumstances themselves and thus the transition from one to the other is, as it were, always at the door; but it need not enter.

What is thus related is linked in a peculiar way. The relation between expressions of life and the world of mind, which governs all understanding, asserts itself here in its most elementary form; according to this, understanding tends towards articulate mental content which becomes its goal; yet the sensually given expressions are not submerged in that content. How, for instance, both the gesture and the terror are not two separate things but a unity, is based on this fundamental relation of expression to mental content. To this must be added the generic character of all the elementary forms of understanding which are to be discussed next.

I have shown how significant the objective mind is for the possibility of knowledge in the human studies. By this I mean the manifold forms in which what individuals hold in common have objectified themselves in the world of the senses.[1] In this objective mind the past is a permanently enduring present for us. Its realm extends from the style of life and the forms of social intercourse, to the system of purposes which society has created for itself, to custom, law, state, religion, art, science and philosophy. For even the work of genius represents ideas, feelings and ideals commonly held in an age and environment. From this world of objective mind the self receives sustenance from earliest childhood. It is the medium in which the understanding of other people and their expressions takes place. For everything in which the mind has objectified itself contains something held in common by the I and the Thou. Every square planted with trees, every room in which seats are arranged, is intelligible to us from our infancy because human planning, arranging and valuing— common to us all—have assigned its place to every square and every object in the room. The child grows up within the order and customs of the family which it shares with the other members and its mother's orders are accepted in this context. Before it learns to talk it is already wholly immersed in that common medium. It learns to understand the gestures and facial expressions, movements and exclamations, words and

[1] For example, as in books or buildings.

sentences, only because it encounters them always in the same form and in the same relation to what they mean and express. Thus the individual orientates himself in the world of objective mind.

From this there follows a consequence important for the process of understanding. The expression of life which the individual grasps is, as a rule, not simply an isolated expression but filled with a knowledge of what is held in common and of a relation to the mental content.

This placing of the individual expressions of life into a common context is facilitated by the articulated order in the objective mind. It embraces particular homogenous systems like law or religion, and these have a firm regular structure. Thus, in civil law, the imperatives enunciated in legal clauses designed to secure what degree of perfection is possible in the conduct of certain human affairs, are related to court-room procedures, law courts and the machinery for carrying out what they decide. Within such a context many kinds of typical differences exist. Thus, the individual expressions of life which confront the understanding subject can be considered as belonging to a common sphere, to a type; and the relationship between the expression of life and the world of mind within that sphere not only places the expression into its context but also supplements the mental content which belongs to it. A sentence is intelligible because a language, the meaning of words and of inflexions, as well as the significance of syntactical arrangements, is common to a community. The fixed order of behaviour within a culture makes it possible for greetings or bows to signify by their nuances a certain mental attitude to other people and to be understood as doing so. In different countries the crafts developed particular procedures and particular instruments for special purposes; when, therefore, the craftsman uses a hammer or saw, his purpose is intelligible to us. In this sphere the relation between expressions of life and mental content is fixed everywhere by a common order. This explains why this relation is present in the grasping of an individual expression and why both links of the process are fused into a unity in the process of understanding, on the basis of the relation between expression and what is expressed, without a conscious reasoning process taking place.

Pages 145-148. Part II. 'The Gradual Elucidation of the Expressions of Life through the Constant Interaction of the two Disciplines' and 'Objectifications of Life'.

The fundamental relation between experience and understanding at which we arrive is that of mutual dependence. More closely determined, it is one of gradual elucidation through the constant interaction of the two classes of truths. The obscurity of experience is illuminated, the mistakes which arise from the narrower comprehension of the subject are corrected, experience itself is widened and completed, in the process of understanding other people—just as other people are understood through our own experience. Understanding constantly widens the range of historical knowledge through the more intensive use of sources, through penetration into a hitherto uncomprehended past and, finally, through the progress of history itself which produces new events and thus widens the very subject of understanding. In this progression such a widening out demands ever new general truths for the comprehension of this world of specific events. The extension of the historical horizon makes the formation of ever more general and more fruitful concepts possible. Thus there arises at every point and at every time in the work of human studies an interaction between experience, understanding and representation of the mind-affected world in general concepts. Every stage of this work has an inner, unified conception of the mind-affected world. For, historical knowledge of specific events, and general truths develop in interaction with each other and are part of the same integral point of view. At every stage understanding of the mind-affected world, from the general idea of it to the methods of criticism and individual investigations, is uniform, or homogenous.

And here we might look back once more to the time in which modern historical consciousness originated. This was when the conceptualizations of the systematic disciplines became consciously based on the study of historical life and when the knowledge of the particular was consciously affected by the systematic disciplines of economics, law, politics and religion. At that point it was possible for methodical insight into the connections of the human studies to arise. The same mind-affected world becomes, according to the different ways of grasping it, the object of two classes of disciplines. Universal history with the unique context of mankind as its subject matter and the system of the independently constituted human studies, of man, language, economics, politics, law, religion and art, supplement each other. They are differentiated by their goals and the methods determined by them and, at the same time, they co-operate constantly in the construction of our knowledge of the mind-affected world . . .

When we have grasped the sum of all the achievements of understanding the objectification of life, in contrast to the subjectivity of experience, opens up within it. Together with experience, the seeing of the objectivity of life (of its externalization in manifold structural systems) becomes the foundation for the human studies. The individual, the communities and the works into which life and mind have entered, form the outer realm of the mind. These manifestations of life, as they present themselves to understanding in the external world, are, as it were, embedded in the context of nature. The great outer reality of the mind always surrounds us. It is a manifestation of the mind in the world of the senses—from the fleeting expression to the century-long rule of a constitution or code of law. *Every single expression of life represents a common feature* in the realm of this objective mind. Every word, every sentence, every gesture or polite formula, every work of art and every historical deed is intelligible because the people who express themselves through them and those who understand them have something in common; the individual always experiences, thinks and acts in a common sphere and only there does he understand. Everything that is understood carries, as it were, the hallmark of familiarity derived from such common features. We live in this atmosphere, it surrounds us constantly. We are immersed in it. We are at home everywhere in this historical and understood world; we understand the sense and meaning of it all; we ourselves are woven into this common sphere.

The changes in expressions of life which affect us challenge us constantly to new understanding; but, because every expression of life and the understanding of it is, at the same time, connected with others, our understanding carries us along naturally from the given particular to the whole. As the relations between what is alike increase, the possibilities of generalization, which already lie in the common features of what is understood, grow.

In understanding, a further characteristic of the objectifications of life asserts itself and determines both the classification according to kinship and the tendency towards generalization. The objectification of life contains in itself an ordered manifold of sub-divisions. From the distinctions of race down to the differences of expressions and customs of a people, or, indeed, of a country town, there exist natural divisions based on mental differences. Differentiations of another kind arise in the cultural systems; yet others distinguish ages from each other; in short; many lines which mark out areas of related life, from some point of view or other, traverse the world of objective mind and cross in it. The recurrence of all these differences helps us to understand the fullness of life expressed in countless nuances.

Only through the idea of the objectification of life do we gain insight into the nature of the historical. Everything in this arose from mental actions and, therefore, bears the hallmark of historicity. From the distribution of trees in a park the arrangement of houses in a street, the functional tool of an artisan, to the sentence pronounced in the courtroom, we are hourly surrounded by the products of history. Whatever characteristics the mind puts into expressions of life today, are, tomorrow, if they persist, history. As time marches on we are surrounded by Roman ruins, cathedrals and the summer castles of autocrats. History is not something separated from life or divided from the present by distance in time.

To summarize. The human studies have as their comprehensive subject matter the objectification of life. But, insofar as this becomes something we understand, it contains the relation of outer to inner. Accordingly, in understanding, this objectification is always related to experience, in which the individual becomes aware of his own mental content and which enables him to interpret that of others. If what is given in the human studies is found in this experience then it is clear that we must abstract from our concept of it everything rigid, everything foreign, which characterizes the picture of the physical world. It is produced by man and, therefore, historical; it is understood and, therefore, contains common features; it is familiar, because understood, and it contains a grouping of the manifold because the interpretation of an expression of life in the higher understanding already rests on such a grouping. The classifying of expressions of life is already rooted in the subject matter of the human studies.

Here the concept of the human studies is completed. Their range is identical with that of understanding and understanding has the objectification of life consistently as its subject matter. Thus the range of the human studies is determined by the objectification of life in the external world. The mind can only understand what it has created. Nature, the subject matter of the natural sciences, embraces the reality which has arisen independently of the activity of the mind. Everything on which man has actively impressed his stamp forms the subject matter of the human studies.

Pages 150-156. Part II. The Objectifications of Life (contd.) and 'The Mind-affected World as a System of Interactions'
But the presuppositions on which Hegel based this concept (of the objective mind) can no longer be retained today. He construed communities from the universal, rational will. Today we must start from the reality of life; in life all the aspects of the mind are involved. Hegel construed metaphysically, we analyse the given. The contemporary analysis of human existence fills us all with a sense of fragility, of the power of dark instinct, of the suffering from obscurities and illusions, of the finitude of all that is life, even where the highest creations of communal life arise from it. Thus we cannot understand the objective mind through reason but must go

back to the structural connections found in living individuals and, by extension, in communities. We cannot place the objective mind into the order of an ideal construction; we must, rather, start with its reality. This we try to understand and to represent in adequate concepts. As the objective mind is thus separated from its one-sided foundation on a universal reason (which expresses the nature of the world spirit) and separated also from any ideal construction, a new conception of it becomes possible; the objective mind embraces language, custom and every form or style of life as well as the family, society, the state and the law. Consequently, what Hegel distinguished from objective mind as absolute mind, namely art, religion and philosophy, also falls under this same concept. In them, particularly, creative individuals show themselves as embodiments of common features and the mind objectifies itself in their powerful personalities and is recognized in them.

This objective mind is differentiated within itself and ranges from mankind down to the most narrowly defined types. This differentiation, the principle of the rise of individuality, is active in it. When the individual is understood on the basis and by means of the universally human, this gives rise to a re-experiencing of the inner connections which lead from the universally human to its individual expressions. This process is grasped in reflection and the psychology of individuality sketches the theory which explains the possibility of the rise of individuality.. The same combination of fundamental regularities and the resultant differentiation into individuals (and, therefore, the combination of general theory and comparative procedure) underlies the systematic human studies. The general truths about moral life or poetry established in the human studies thus become the foundation for insight into the differences between various moral ideals and poetic activities.

Past ages, in which the great total forces of history have taken shape, are present in the objective mind. The individual, as bearer and representative of the general features interwoven in him, enjoys and grasps the history in which they arose. He understands history because he himself is a historical being.

In one last point the concept of objective mind here developed diverges from that of Hegel. Insofar as life in its totality (experience, understanding, historical context of life and power of the irrational) takes the place of Hegel's 'Reason', the problem of how the science of history is possible arises. For Hegel this problem did not exist. His metaphysic (in which the world spirit with nature as its manifestation, the objective mind as its actualization and the absolute mind, culminating in philosophy, as the realization of the knowledge of it, are in themselves identical) has left this problem behind. But, today, the task is the reverse—to recognize the actual historical expressions of life as the true foundation of historical knowledge and to find a method of answering the question how, on the basis of what is thus given, universally valid knowledge of the historical world is possible.

In experience and understanding the mind-affected world unfolds before us through the objectifications of life. We must now determine more closely the nature of this mind-affected world (the historical and social world) as the object of the human studies. Let us first summarize the results of the preceding investigations about the interrelatedness of the human studies. This interrelatedness rests on the relationship between experience and understanding and here three main principles emerged. The extension of our knowledge of what is given in experience takes place through the interpretation of the objectifications of life and this interpretation, in turn, is only made possible by plumbing the depths of subjective experience. In the same way the understanding of the particular is only possible because knowledge of the general is present in it and this, in turn, presupposes understanding. Finally, the understanding of a part of the historical course of events only reaches completion through the relation of the part to the whole and a universal-historical survey of the whole presupposes the understanding of the parts united in it.

As a result, the comprehension of every particular state of affairs of the human studies within the common historical whole and the comprehension of the conceptual representation of this whole in the systematic human studies are mutu-

ally dependent.[1] The interaction of experience and understanding in the comprehension of the mind-affected world,
the mutual dependence of general and particular knowledge
and, finally, the gradual illumination of the mind-affected
world in the progress of the human studies, appear at every
point of their development. Therefore, we find them again in
all the operations of the human studies. They form the
universal foundation of their structure. Thus we shall have
to recognize the interdependence of interpretation, criticism,
linking of sources, and synthesis into a historical whole. A
similar relation exists in the formation of the concepts of such
subjects as economics, law, philosophy, art and religion which
refer to the interactions of different persons in a common
task. In scientific conceptualization determination of the
characteristics of a concept always presupposes the ascertaining of the facts which are to be subsumed under it; and for
the ascertaining and selecting of these facts characteristics
are required which indicate that they fall within the range of
the concept. To determine the concept of poetry I must
extract it from all the facts covered by it and, to ascertain
which works belong to poetry, I must already be aware of a
characteristic by means of which I can recognize a work as
poetical.

This relation is, therefore, the most general feature of the
structure of the human studies.

Thus we come to understand the mind-affected world as a
system of interactions or as an interrelationship contained in
its enduring creations. The subject matter of the human
studies lies in this system of interactions and its creations.
They analyse either that system of interactions, or the logical,
aesthetic or religious system embodied in a stable form
appropriate to each, or, finally, the system contained in a constitution or law-book (which points back to the system of
interactions from which it originated).[2]

[1] In other words, to understand the relevance of economic conditions
to a historical event involves a knowledge of the relevance of Economics to History.
[2] The economic system, for example, can be seen either in terms of
activities such as producing, selling, etc., or as a net of relationships
between organizations, firms and factories.

This system of interactions is distinguished from the causal order of nature by the fact that, in accordance with the structure of mental life, it creates *values* and realizes *purposes*; and this, not occasionally, not here and there; for the mind is so structured as to produce them through the system of interactions and comprehension. I call this the immanent teleological character of the system of interactions of the mind. By this I mean an interaction inherent in the structure of a dynamic system. Historical life is creative; it constantly produces goods and values and all concepts of these are reflections of its activity.

This constant creation of values and goods in the mind-affected world proceeds from individuals and communities and cultural systems in which the individuals co-operate. This co-operation is determined by the fact that, for the realization of values, they subject themselves to rules and set themselves purposes. Thus every form of co-operation is based on qualities in human nature which link individuals together—on a core, as it were, which cannot be understood in terms of psychology but expresses itself in every such system of relations between human beings. Any achievement is determined by the structural connections between comprehension and the psychological states expressed firstly, in valuation and, secondly, in the positing of purposes, goods and standards. Such a system of interactions operates primarily in individuals. They are, thus, the crossing points of systems of relations, each of which is a continual source of activity. Consequently, in each system common goods and orderly procedures for their realization are developed; unconditional validity is then attributed to them. In every permanent relationship between individuals a development in which values, rules and purposes are produced, made conscious and consolidated by processes of thought, takes place. This productive activity which occurs in individuals, communities, cultural systems and nations under natural conditions which constantly provide material and stimulation, achieves self-consciousness in the human studies.

Furthermore, it is in the nature of the structural system that every unit of the world of the mind has its centre within itself. Like the individual every cultural system, every community, has a focal point within itself. In it, a conception of reality, valuation, and production of goods, are linked into a whole.

A new fundamental relation in the system of interactions, the subject matter of the human studies, now stands revealed. The different units from which creative activity proceeds are woven into wider social-historical contexts; these are nations, ages, historical periods. Thus, complex forms of historical connections arise. The values, purposes and links which, sustained by individuals, communities and systems of relations, occur in them, must be brought together by the historian. He compares them, lifts out what is common to them and synthesizes the various systems of interactions; and, from the centring on itself of every historical unit, there arises a different form of unity. What is simultaneous and interacts—such as individuals, cultural systems or communities—stands in constant communication with, and thus supplements its own life directly through that of others; nations are often relatively self-contained and, because of this, have their own horizon; but, if I now consider the period of the Middle Ages I find that its horizon is distinct from that of previous periods. Even where the results of these periods persist they are assimilated into the system of the medieval world. *It has a closed horizon.* Thus an epoch is *centred* on itself *in a new sense.* The common practices of an epoch become the norm for the activities of the individuals in it. The pattern of the systems of interaction of the society of an epoch has constant features. Within it the relations in the comprehension of objects show an inner affinity. The ways of feeling, the inner life and the impulses which arise from it, are similar to each other. The will, too, chooses similar goals, strives for related goods and finds itself committed in a similar way. It is the task of historical analysis to discover the climate which governs the concrete purposes, values and ways of thought of a period. Even the contrasts which prevail there are determined by this common background. Thus, every action, every thought, every common activity, in short, every part of this historical whole, has its significance through its relation to the whole of the epoch or age. And when the historian judges, he ascertains what the individual has achieved within this context and how far his vision and activity may have extended beyond it.

The historical world as a whole, this whole as a system of interactions, this system of interactions as a source of values and purposes, (that is, as creative), the understanding of this whole from within itself, and, finally, the centring of values and purposes in ages, epochs, and in universal history, these are the points of view from which the projected system of the human studies must be considered. Thus science, in accordance with its tendency towards universal validity, gradually replaces the direct relation between life, its values and purposes, and the subject matter of history by insight into the immanent relationships which exist in the system of inter-actions of the historical world, between productive power, values, purposes, meaning and significance. Only on the basis of such objective history do the questions arise; is prediction of the future possible and, if so, how far? and; can our lives be subordinated to the common goals of mankind?

The comprehension of the system of interactions arises, primarily, in the experiencing subject for whom the sequence of inner events unfolds in structural relations. These con-nections are then rediscovered in other individuals through understanding. Thus the fundamental form of the connections arises in the individual who combines present, past and pos-sibilities of the future into the course of his life. This also has its place in the historical process in which different lives are co-ordinated. When the wider context of an event is observed by a spectator or reported in an account, the conception of historical events arises; and, as the individual events occupy a position in the course of time (which presupposes productive forces from the past and an effect on the future) every event demands a sequel and the present leads into the future.

Another kind of context prevails in works which, separated from their authors, have their own life and are a law unto themselves. Before we penetrate to the system of inter-actions in which they originated we must grasp the connec-tions which are there in the completed work. In the under-standing the logical connections through which legal principles are linked into a code of law emerge. If we read one of Shakespeare's comedies we find the component parts of an event linked according to relations of time and causality and elevated into unity according to the laws of poetical composition; and this unity lifts the beginning and the end out of the causal chain and links its parts into a whole.

CHAPTER V

THE HISTORICAL APPROACH AND
THE ORDER OF THE HUMAN WORLD

In developing a methodology of the understanding of individuals Dilthey was laying the foundations for his theory of historical understanding. History is concerned with human beings and deals with physical facts only so far as they affect human life. Indeed, it is the task of history to show what man is. The methods of understanding human beings are, therefore, obviously relevant to it. But how are they to be applied? A person is a natural unit existing continuously from birth to death. He has a limited range of experiences and interprets them in his own way. He has ideals and pursues aims; he may develop and progress in wisdom or skill and his memory is cumulative. Thus we have here a unified subject matter, the facts are pre-selected for us and a pattern which we can recapture has emerged. But history is not about any one individual or—and here Dilthey decisively rejects Hegel—any superindividual who has aims and purposes, who remembers and makes progress. From what, then, do we start in history? How do we arrive at a manageable subject matter? How do we select the relevant and where do we find patterns which make a conceptual grasp possible?

The history of historiography shows us concretely how the historian's craft developed. Dilthey has dealt extensively with this subject and particularly with the historical movements of the nineteenth century. In the text I have included one of his briefer accounts. History starts with simple narration and proceeds to a deeper psychological insight into the minds of the historical actors and to a growing awareness of patterns of interactions such as the interweaving of economic, political, social and military factors. Gradually the idea of universal history emerges and the concept of development is applied to it. Finally, we get the breaking up of the historical context into specialized spheres such as those of religion, art or economics. This development embodies the practical answers historians have given to the questions set out above. Dilthey developed the methodological implications of their achievements.

The historian must start from objective evidence, from eye-witness accounts and from remnants of the past, such as buildings, coins and, above all, letters, diaries and state papers, which will stand up to historical scepticism. The possibility of historical reconstruction depends on the extent to which material of this kind is available. But the material must be sifted critically to ascertain the genuineness of remains and the reliability of reports. Here we encounter, once more, the need for a kind of shuttlecock movement. The general picture of the past must be based on the collation of individual pieces of evidence yet the reliability and genuineness of each piece of evidence can only be established in the light of that general picture of the past.

We can reconstruct the pattern of past events from the evidence by applying to it our understanding of human nature and the knowledge embodied in the systematic human studies. It is a reconstruction, and not simply a construction, because we find that the phenomena of the past have a unity and a pattern of their own and even present us with principles of selection. Great historical events, such as the rise of Christianity or the French revolution, are characterized by special combinations of forces active in them. These forces are of a kind familiar in our lives and they may be classified into two groups. There are 'negative forces' such as the pressure of circumstances, the needs and wants prevalent in an age and there are 'positive forces' such as the ideals, creative urges and will to power which moved the actors in any historical situation.

In his understanding of these forces the historian is greatly aided by the fact that they tend to become objectified into systems and organizations. Such objectifications are universities, churches, political parties, industries, scientific institutes and legal systems. Individuals are variously related to these systems. Through them they cope with their circumstances and pursue their goals. They are influenced by them and receive something from them. These structures have a kind of life of their own. They have their own history and tradition (possibly embodied in records) their defined function or purposes, sometimes their own property and their own sphere of activity. Because they are functional embodiments of one human purpose or another (or group of purposes) they are rationally comprehensible and may even exhibit orderly development.

The state, too, is such a system, its function being the organization of power. But it is different from the others because it is the comprehensive framework for all the other systems and may even take over some of their functions, such as education or industrial production.

When an aggregate of human beings is organized by means of these different systems within the framework of the state, we get a nation. The life of a nation shows recognizable continuity in different manifestations, in religion, art, legal system and economic structure, because its citizens are all exposed to similar conditions, share a common tradition and participate in the different social and cultural spheres. (The same person may be an economic entrepreneur, a church warden and a poet). Thus, the life of a nation is centred around common beliefs, ideals, purposes and ways of doing things in terms of which it can be understood. But Dilthey expressly rejects the notion, associated, for instance, with the Marxist view of history, that the continuity in a nation's life is due to the fact that one system, such as the economic one, is the basis of all the others.

What Dilthey says about nations also applies to periods or ages. They, too, exhibit, and for the same kind of reasons, pervasive features and common ideas which extend beyond national boundaries. Further continuity is provided by the dynamic relations between such historical periods. Each of them arises out of the tensions and contradiction, as well as the creative energies, of previous ages.

These systems and organizations, states, nations and ages are the units which form the subject matter of the historian. Because they embody human ideas and purposes historical understanding can be applied to them. But, in what sense can we talk of nations or states as subjects to which continued existence, purposes and activities can be attributed? Dilthey rejects categorically any notion that they are the embodiments of such superindividual entities as collective wills or national souls. There are only individual human beings who feel, think and act. But he also rejects any attempt to eliminate the notions of corporate purposes and actions. He considers it a matter of empirical fact that individuals pursue collective purposes and act in common causes.

The various units (cultural systems, nations, states) have structures of their own and are complexly interrelated with each other. Hence they provided the historian with intelligible patterns which his research can recapture. These patterns do not, of course, constitute the unfolding of a rational idea. Everywhere in history there are brute facts, chance and irrational striving. But, because human beings have tried everywhere, by organized endeavour, to cope with these, the historian can, at every point, discover pattern and meaning.

TEXT

Pages 252-253.   Part III.   History
The firm links within autobiography now vanish. We leave the river of the course of a life and the infinite sea receives us.

On this wide sea we take with us the aids to orientation which we have acquired from experience, understanding, autobiography and biography. They are the historical categories which have arisen from reflection on life to be the intellectual tools for comprehending it. In the understanding the category of the whole is already given. The passage of time—the course of a life—shows the relatedness of parts in a whole. In biography the category of the qualitatively determined individual existence arises. As the individual existence is conditioned from the outside and reacts outwards the categories of action and suffering are given in it. Every individual in history is a power and interacts with other powers. Individual existence unfolds in the course of a life; the limitations experienced in its different moments result in suffering, pressure, and progress to a state more congenial at the time; in this progress the individual finds happiness; perhaps happiness even consists of this; thus the individual existence continues as itself and, at the same time, changes with every circumstance. The law operative within the individual regulates this change and what has been acquired determines the future from within. From all this arise the categories of essence and development. Here essence only refers to persistence during change and development only to the form of a course of events determined by the law of a progressively acquired context. The experience or comprehension of an individual does not tell us anything about development in the sense of progress.[1]

To look back. Inner connections exist between the categories which are particularly characteristic of the human studies.

The relations between them form these connections and hence the qualitatively determined existence of an individual can be understood through them. Through these relations we now grasp the context in which we understand a given reality according to its meaning.

Page 311. Part IV. The Task
They, [the human studies] also contain states of affairs which cannot be experienced or understood inwardly, namely the physical facts. History describes the tumult and noise of battles, the disposition of opposing armies, the effectiveness of their artillery, the influence of the terrain on the outcome. Here, as everywhere in the course of history, physical events, what they make necessary and the effects which originate from them, are an important part of the description. But they belong to history only insofar as they determine the develop-

[1] See footnote 1, page 105.

ment of individuals or associations of individuals, or because they are considered by the individuals or communities in the choice of means for ends, or influence the success of their actions; in brief, in relation to what can be inwardly experienced or understood. The same relation appears in the systematic human studies. Settlement on a piece of land is dependent on the relation between its yield and the labour involved. But how the composition of the soil on which this relation is dependent varies, interests the economist only insofar as it stands in relation to need, labour, satisfaction; in brief, to what is known in experience and in the understanding of that experience, or in judgements and concepts about it.

Pages 279-280. Part III. The Historical Concept

Man knows himself only in history, never through introspection; indeed, we all seek him in history. Or, to put it more generally, we seek what is human in it, such as religion, and so on. We want to know what it is. If there were a science of man it would be anthropology which aims at understanding the totality of experience through the structural context. The individual always realizes only one of the possibilities in his development, which could always have taken a different turning whenever he had to make an important decision. Man is only given to us at all in terms of his realized possibilities. In the cultural systems, too, we seek an anthropologically determined structure in which an 'x' realizes himself. We call this human nature but this is only a word for a conceptual system constituted by an intellectual method.[1] The possibilities of man are not exhausted by this either.

The horizon widens. Even if the historian has a limited subject in front of him a thousand threads lead on and on into the infinity of all the memories of mankind. Historiography begins retracing its steps from the present with the description of what is still alive in the memory of the present generation. It is still recollection in the proper sense. Or, annals, added to year by year, record what has just happened. As

---

[1] Modern cultural anthropology tends to confirm Dilthey's view that what we call human nature is usually a culturally determined realization of certain human potentialities.

history advances vision extends beyond one's own country and more and more of the past enters into the shadow world of memory. Expressions of it all have remained after life itself has passed away; direct expressions in which souls expressed what they were and also accounts of deeds, circumstances of individuals, communities and states. And the historian stands in the midst of the ruins, of the remnants of things past, the expressions of minds in deeds, words, sounds and pictures, of souls who have long ceased to be. How is he to conjure them up? All his work of recalling them is interpretation of the remnants which remain. Imagine a person who had no memory of his own past but only thought and acted through what the past had wrought in him, without being conscious of any of its parts. This would be the state of nations, communities, of mankind itself, if it were not possible to supplement the remnants, to interpret the expressions, to lift the accounts of deeds from isolation back into the context in which they originated. All this is interpretation, a hermeneutic art.

The problem is what form it assumes when it is wholly separated from individual existence, when assertions are to be made about subjects which are associations of people in some sense or other, about cultural systems, nations or states.

First of all, we require a method for discovering firm lines of demarcation within the infinite interactions of individuals, where the unity of personal life provides no frontiers. It is as if we had to draw permanent lines and figures on an ever-running stream. Between this reality and reason no relation of comprehension seems possible, for the concept separates what is connected in the flow of life and represents something which is valid, independent of the person who expresses it, something that is universal and for ever. But the flow of life is everywhere unique, every wave in it rises and dies away.

Pages 161-162. Part II. Historical Knowledge
The comprehension of the system of interactions of history grows first of all from individual points at which remnants of the past belonging together are linked in understanding by their relation to experience; what is near and around us

becomes a means of understanding what is distant and past. The condition for this interpretation of historical remnants is that what we put into them must be constant and universally valid. On the basis of the connections which the historian has experienced within himself he transfers his knowledge of customs, habits, political circumstances and religious processes to these remnants. The germinal cell of the historical world is the experience in which the subject discovers himself in dynamic relationship with his environment. The environment acts on the subject and is acted upon by him. It is composed of the physical and cultural surroundings. In every part of the historical world there exists, therefore, the same dynamic connection between a course of mental events and an environment. Hence there arises the task of evaluating the influences of nature on man and of ascertaining the impact of his cultural environment on him.

Just as raw materials in industry are subjected to various forms of processing so are the remnants of the past brought to full historical understanding through different procedures. Criticism, interpretation and synthesis of the understanding of a historical process interlock. But here, too, it is characteristic that one operation is not simply based on another; criticism, interpretation and intellectual synthesis differ in their tasks; but the accomplishment of each of these tasks always demands insights gained from the others.

It follows from this relationship that the explanation of historical connections is always dependent on an interrelation of acts which is never fully describable and, therefore, cannot justify itself by incontestable proofs when confronted with historical scepticism. We have only to think of Niebuhr's[1] great discoveries about older Roman history. His criticism is everywhere inseparable from his reconstruction of the true course of events. He had to ascertain how the existing tradition of older Roman history came about and what conclusions about its historical value could be drawn from its origin. At the same time he had to try to deduce the real historical course of events from what could be argued from the facts.

[1] Barthold George Niebuhr, 1776-1831. Pioneer of historical source criticism.

No doubt this methodical procedure moves in a circle if one applies the rules of strict demonstration to it.[1] And when Niebuhr availed himself, at the same time, of an analogical argument from similar developments, the knowledge of these related developments was subject to the same circle and the analogical argument which made use of it produced no compelling certainty.

Even in contemporary accounts we must first examine the point of view of the reporter, his reliability, and his relation to the event. And the further removed from the time of the events the accounts are, the less their credibility, unless the value of the elements of such an account can be ascertained by tracing them back to older reports contemporary to the event. The history of the ancient world has secure foundations where original sources exist, and that of the newer one where documents which portray the course of a historical event are preserved. Therefore, certain knowledge of political history began only with the methodical and critical collections of documents and with historians getting free access to archives.

This knowledge can, as far as the facts are concerned, stand up to historical scepticism and, on such secure foundations, a reconstruction which has historical probability (and to which only clever but unscientific minds can deny usefulness) can be built up by analysing the sources of the accounts and examining the points of view of the reporters. This reconstruction, indeed, does not achieve certain knowledge of the motives of the actors, but of the actions and events and the errors about individual facts to which we remain exposed do not cast doubt on the whole.

Historiography, where it deals with mass phenomena, or, above all, where it confronts artistic or scientific works which stand up to analysis, is much more favourably placed than when trying to comprehend the course of political events.

---

[1] In other words—to evaluate the evidence available he has to consider whether it corresponds to what happened, but he only knows what happened from the available evidence.

Page 261. Part III. The Possibility of an Objective Know-
ledge in the Human Studies
The first condition for the construction of the historical world
is, therefore, the purification, by means of criticism and interpretation, of the confused and often corrupt memories of
mankind about itself. Therefore, the fundamental science for
history is philology in its formal sense implying the scientific
study of language in which tradition has been preserved, the
collection of the literary remains of mankind up to the present
time, the elimination of errors from them and the chrono-
logical ordering and combining which places these documents
into inner relations. Philology, in this sense, is not just an aid
to the historian but indicates the range of procedures he must
use first.

Pages 163-171. Part II. Stages of Historical Understanding.
The Mind-affected World as a System of Interactions
The mastering of historical material takes place in various
stages which gradually penetrate into the depths of history.

Manifold interests lead, first of all, to narration of what has
occurred. Here, above all, an original need is satisfied—
curiosity about human affairs, particularly about those of
one's native land. In addition, pride in nation and state asserts
itself. Thus the narrative art originates and Herodotus is the
model for all succeeding ages. Now the tendency towards
explanation steps into the foreground. The Athenian culture
of the time of Thucydides first provided the right conditions
for it. Actions were traced back by acute observation to their
psychological motives; the struggles of the states for power
and their course and outcome, are explained in terms of their
military and political strength; the effects of constitutions are
studied. As a great political thinker like Thucydides elucidates
the past through the sober study of the dynamic interactions
in it, we see that history also illuminates the future. When a
former course of interactions is comprehended and when the
first stages of an event are like it, the occurrence of a similar
sequel can be expected on the basis of an analogical argument.
This argument, on which Thucydides bases the lessons of
history for the future, is, indeed, of decisive significance for

political thought. As in the natural sciences, so also in history, a regularity in the pattern of interactions makes prediction and intervention based on knowledge possible. The contemporaries of the Sophists already studied constitutions as political forces; then Polybius confronts us with historiography in which the *methodical application of the systematic* human studies to the *explanation* of the historical context makes it possible to introduce the effect of permanent forces like the constitution, military organization, and fiscal system, into the explanatory procedure. The subject matter of Polybius was the interaction between states which, from the beginning of the struggle between Rome and Carthage up to the destruction of Carthage and Corinth, formed the historical world for the European mind. Polybius undertakes the task of deducing individual political events from the study of the permanent forces in these states. Thus his point of view becomes that of universal history because he combined within himself Greek theoretical culture, study of the cunning politics and warfare of his native land and a knowledge of Rome which only intercourse with leading statesmen of the new universal state could provide. Manifold cultural forces now become active in the period from Polybius to Machiavelli and Guicciardini,[1] above all, the infinite deepening of self-knowledge and the simultaneous widening of the historical horizon; but the two great Italian historians certainly remain close to Polybius in their methods.

Only in the eighteenth century was a new stage of historiography reached. Two great principles were then introduced successively; the concrete pattern of interactions lifted by the historian as subject matter from the great stream of history was *divided up into individual* contexts like those of law, religion, poetry, embraced by the unity of an age. This presupposes that the eye of the historian looks beyond political history to that of culture, that the function of each sphere of culture has been understood by the systematic human studies, and that an understanding of the co-operation of such cultural systems has grown. The new historiography began in the age

---

[1] Francesco Guicciardini, 1483-1540. Italian statesman and historian; friend of Machiavelli.

of Voltaire. From Winkelmann,[1] Justus Möser[2] and Herder[3] onwards a second principle, that of development, was added. This asserts that a new fundamental characteristic is contained in a historical course of interactions, namely that, according to its inner nature, it traverses a series of changes each of which is only possible on the basis of the previous one.

These different stages designate elements which, once grasped, have remained alive in historiography. Joyful narrative art, penetrating explanation, application of systematic knowledge to it, dissection into individual systems of interactions and the principle of development are combined and strengthen each other.

The significance of analysing the concrete system of interactions and scientifically synthesizing its individual systems has emerged more and more clearly.

The historian does not follow up the nexus of events from one point in all directions into infinity; for, in the unity of subject matter which forms the theme of the historian, there lies the principle of selection, which is present in the task of comprehending just this particular subject. Not only does the treatment of the historical subject demand that it should be singled out from the breadth of the concrete system of interactions; the subject also contains a principle of selection. The fall of Rome, or the liberation of the Netherlands, or the French revolution, demand the selection of such events and connections as contain (in the case of the dissolution of the Roman empire, the liberation of the Netherlands, the carrying out of the revolution) the causes, both particular and general, and all the forms which the active forces took. The historian who deals with systems of interactions must select and connect in such a way that those familiar with the details miss

[1] Johann Joachim Winkelmann, 1717-1768. German archaeologist and art-historian who helped to revive admiration for Greek art. Friend of Goethe.
[2] Justus Möser, 1720-1794. Statesman, publicist and historian interested in local history.
[3] Johann Gottfried von Herder, 1744-1803. Poet and writer. Exercised great influence on the development of the Philosophy of History, aesthetics and the study of folk poetry. Friend of Goethe.

nothing, because each of them is represented in features of the total system of interactions. In this lies his descriptive art, which is also a product of a special way of seeing. When we examine these strong, pervasive connections we see again how insight into them springs from the combination of progressive historical understanding of sources and ever deeper comprehension of the connections of mental life. If, then, we look more closely at the kind of system of interactions encountered in the greatest events of history, the development of Christianity, the Reformation, the French revolution, the national wars of liberation, we can grasp it as the formation of a total force which, moving in one direction, overthrows all resistance. We shall always find that two kinds of forces co-operate in it. Some are tensions which derive from the sense of urgent, unfulfilled needs, from desire of all kinds prompted by them, from an increase of frictions and struggles, and, also, from the consciousness of an insufficiency of power to defend the status quo. Others arise from the dynamic energy of a positive will, potency and faith. They rest on the vigorous instincts of many but are illuminated and heightened by the experiences of great personalities. And, as these positive tendencies grow from the past and direct themselves towards the future, they are creative. They contain ideals in the form of enthusiasm and this has a special way of communicating and spreading itself.

From this we deduce the general principle that, in the system of interactions of the great events of the world, the conditions of pressure and tension and the feeling of the insufficiency of the existing state of affairs—that is negative emotions of rejection—form the basis for the action which is sustained by positive valuations, desirable goals and ends. The great changes of the world originate in the co-operation of these two. The real agents in the system of interactions are the mental states which can be formulated in terms of value, good and purpose; among these states not only the tendencies towards cultural goods but also the will to power, culminating in the inclination to subjugate others, must be considered as active forces.

Thus it becomes clear that the determination of the subject

matter of a historical work involves a selection of events and connections. Because the concrete system of interactions in history is made up systematically of individual distinguishable spheres of activity the actions of individuals directed towards a common achievement form a uniform and homogenous system of interactions. I have discussed this relation before.[1] On it, conceptualization, through which connections of a general character can be grasped in historical reasearch, is based. The analysis and isolating by which such systems of interactions are separated out is, therefore, the decisive procedure which the logical dissection of the human studies has to examine. The relationship of this analysis to that in which the structural system of individual minds is discovered, is obvious.

The simplest and most homogenous systems of interactions which bring a cultural achievement into being are education, economic life, law, politics, religions, social life, art, philosophy, science. I shall now bring out the characteristics of such a system.

Productive acts take place in it. Thus, the law realizes the enforceable conditions for the perfection of the conditions of life. It is the nature of poetry to express experience and to describe objectifications of life in such a way that the event singled out by the poet is represented effectively as meaningful for the whole of life. In such productive activity individuals are connected with each other. Their individual processes are related to the system of productive interactions and belong to it. Thus, these processes are links in a system which bring about a certain result.

The statutes of the legal code, the action in which parties contend before a court about some inheritance—in accordance with the rules of that code—the decision of the court and its implementation; what a long series of mental processes we have here; among how many people they can be distributed; how variously they interact in order, finally, to solve the legal problem involved in the human situation before us.

The writing of poetry is, to a much higher degree, bound

[1] See page 129.

up with the single process in the poet's soul; but no poet is the exclusive creator of his works; he takes over an event from oral tradition, he finds already in existence the epic form in which he elevates it to poetry, he studies the effect of individual scenes in predecessors, he uses a certain metre, he receives his idea of the meaning of life from popular views or from outstanding individuals, and he needs the receiving, enjoying listener who absorbs his verses and so realizes his dream of making an impression. Thus the achievements of the law, poetry, or any other teleological system of culture are realized in a system of interactions which consists of certain processes in certain individuals being linked together to bring it about.

In the system of interactions of a cultural system a second characteristic asserts itself. Apart from his function in the legal system the judge stands in other, different, systems of interactions; he acts in the interests of his family; he has to perform some economic activity; he exercises his political function; perhaps he also writes verse. Thus, it is not the complete individual that is linked to such a system of interactions; but only those processes in him which belong to a certain system are related to each other within that system and the individual is woven into different systems of interactions.

The system of interactions of such a cultural sphere is realized through the differentiated functions of its constituent parts. The firm scaffolding of each system is formed by people for whom the processes which serve the activity are the main business of life—be it from inclination or be it from a combination of inclination and vocation. Among them the people who, as it were, embody in themselves the resolution to achieve these results and are made into representatives of this cultural system by a combination of talent and vocation, stand out. The productive activity in such a field is, in the last resort, sustained by the creative natures, the founders of religions, the discoverers of a new philosophic view of the world, the scientific inventors.

Thus there is interdependence in such a system of interactions; widespread accumulated tensions press towards the satisfaction of needs; productive energy finds the path along which satisfaction is reached or it produces the creative idea which leads society on; successors as well as recipients then join in.

To continue the analysis; every cultural system which achieves something realizes a common value for all those who concern themselves with that activity. What the individual needs, and yet can never realize, he receives through the productive activity of the community—a jointly created, comprehensive value, in which he can participate. The individual needs his life, his property, his family connections to be secure; but it is only the independent power of the community that satisfies his needs by maintaining enforceable rules of co-existence which make the protection of these goods possible. On the primitive levels the individual suffers from the pressure of ungovernable forces which surround him outside the narrow circle of the activities of his tribe or nation; but lessening of this pressure is brought about only by the creation of faith through the communal spirit. In every cultural system of this kind an order of values arises from the nature of the activity which the system of interactions serves; it is created by the common work for it; objectifications of life, the distillation of human labour, arise in the form of organizations which bring about the achievements in the cultural systems—legal books, philosophic and poetic works. The good which the achievement was to bring into being now exists and is constantly being perfected.

The parts of such a system of interactions acquire significance through their relation to the whole which sustains values and purposes. To start with, the parts of a life have a meaning according to their relation to that life, its values and purposes, and according to the place they occupy in it. Furthermore, historical events become significant through being links in a system of interactions in which they co-operate with other parts to bring about values and purposes in the whole.

While we face the complex connections of historical events in perplexity and can perceive in them neither structure, regularities nor development, we can see a structure peculiar to it in every system of interactions which brings about a cultural achievement. If we see philosophy as such a system of interactions it presents itself first of all as a multiplicity of achievements; sublimation of views of the world into universal validity, reflection on knowledge itself, reference of our purposive activities and practical knowledge to the system of knowledge, a spirit of criticism which is present in the whole of culture, synthesis and justification. But historical research proves that here we are dealing with functions which, though they occur under historical conditions, rest ultimately on the same philosophic basis. It is universal reflection which thus proceeds towards the highest generalizations and final explanations. Hence, the structure of philosophy lies in the relation between this fundamental tendency and the individual functions governed by the circumstances of the age. Thus metaphysics develops everywhere in the inner connection between life, experience of life and a view of the world. As the desire for firm foundations for ever struggling against the chanciness of our lives finds no lasting satisfaction in the religious and poetical forms of a view of the world, we try to raise such a view of the world to universally valid knowledge. Furthermore, in every case we can find differentiation into individual forms in the system of interactions of a cultural sphere.[1]

Every cultural system, because of its achievement, its structure and its regularity has a development. While no law of development can be discovered in the concrete course of events, analysing it into individual, homogenous, systems of interactions reveals sequences of states which are inwardly determined and presuppose each other, so that a higher level raises itself on the basis of a low and progressive differentiation and synthesis takes place.[2]

Each of the states of the civilized world and, above all, the nations developed on the basis of the natural divisions of mankind and the historical process, unites dynamic systems of culture within itself. Our analysis is to be confined to this typical form of present day political organization.

[1] i.e., Different philosophic systems.
[2] In other words we can trace the development of science, or of the postal services, but it is doubtful if we can talk usefully about the development of mankind.

Each of these states is an organization of different communities. What ultimately links them together is the sovereign power of the state beyond which there is no appeal. And who can deny that the meaning of history, founded as it is on life, expresses itself as much in the will to power, in the lust for internal and external dominion which fills these states, as in the cultural systems? And to all this brutality, terror and destruction contained in the will to power, with all the pressure and compulsion which lies in the relationship between internal rule and obedience, is there not linked the consciousness of community, of belonging together, of joyful participation in the power of the political whole (experiences which belong to the highest human values)? The complaint about the brutality of state power is strange; for, as Kant already saw, the heaviest task of mankind lies in the fact that individual self-will, and its striving to expand the sphere of its power and enjoyment, must be tamed by the collective will and the compulsion exercised by it; that, further, if such collective wills conflict only war can bring a decision and, finally, that even within the state compulsion is the last court of appeal. The conditions which make the cultural systems possible at all arise on the basis of the will to power inherent in political organizations. Thus a composite structure occurs. In it the organization of power and interrelated purposive systems are linked into a higher unity. Common features arise in it, first of all, through the interaction of the cultural systems. For the purpose of illustration I shall go back to the oldest accessible Teutonic society as Caesar and Tacitus describe it. Here, as in every later period, we find economic life, state and law linked to language, myth, religiousness and poetry. Between the characteristics of the individual spheres of life there exists an interaction which pervades the whole at any given time. Thus heroic poetry, which had already celebrated Arminius, arose from the warlike spirit in the Teutonic age of Tacitus and this poetry, in its turn, invigorated the warlike spirit. From this same warlike spirit inhumanity arose in the religious sphere, as in the sacrifice of prisoners and the hanging up of their corpses in sacred places. The same spirit then affected the position of the god of war in the world of the gods and this again reacted on the warlike attitude. Thus there arises so strong an agreement between the different spheres of life that we can draw conclusions from the conditions in one about those in another. But this interaction does not fully explain the common features which link the different achievements of a nation. Nor does the uniformity and harmony between economic life, warfare, constitution law, language, myth, religiousness and poetry in this age spring from the fact that one fundamental function, like economic life or military activity, conditions the others. Neither can that uniformity and harmony be deduced as the product of the interaction of the different spheres as they existed then. Put generally, whatever effects proceeded from the strength and character of certain achievements, the kinship which links the different spheres of life within a nation originates, above all, from common depths which no description can exhaust. They exist for us only in the expressions of life which emerge from and express them. At any given time it is the individual human being in a nation who puts something of his own individuality into every expression of life in a certain sphere of culture; for the elements of individual lives which are combined in a system of achievements do not, as we saw, arise exclusively from that system; the whole person is always active in each of his occupations and imparts his own characteristics to them. And, as the state organization embraces various communities down to the family, the wide circle of national life includes smaller contexts and communities which have their own impetus; and all these systems of interactions cross in individuals. In addition the state takes over the activity of the cultural systems; Frederick's Prussia is the most extreme and comprehensive type of state activity. Beside the independent forces which continue to operate in the cultural systems the state is also active; in the processes of a state independent activity goes hand in hand with dependence on the whole.

Pages 282-285. Part III. The Nations. National History
Here, [in the case of nations] the subject which experiences inwardly the unity and significance of outer events in terms

of meaning, value and purpose, is not present in the same way as in the case of the individual; also the subject which experiences is not the same as that which comprehends; for the individual confronts the nation as a spectator even when he belongs to it.[1] Because of this, understanding, through the categories peculiar to it, becomes something different.

The question of how the subject (a people, a nation) is to be delimited as a reality—a question which is quite different from the one of how the subject is experienced—can be illuminated only in the sense that the *concepts themselves and their delimitations are historically relative*. The unity of the subject, a people, is quite variable according to the elements which constitute it. When was German national unity achieved? In the Middle Ages the unity of language is only relative, because of the difference of dialects in the tribes. By nation we understand a stable, economic, social and political combination of parts.

But it is the relation between the factually based unity of the subject and the consciousness of belonging together, of nationality and national feeling, on which the unity of the subject finally rests.

This consciousness of belonging together is conditioned by the same elements that assert themselves in the individual's consciousness of himself.

Some experiences are felt to concern everybody. This is also the case in a teleological system, for example, a religious organization. But this communal feeling is present only in a certain class of experience. In a nation, however, all sorts of common experiences stand in conscious relation to the community. This community refers to all aspects of the lives of the individuals who belong to it. The result is that every great experience is felt as something affecting the values of the community. That purposes which belong to this national context are formed is an expression of that same consciousness of belonging together. For all these individuals—each of

[1] If Britain passes through an economic crisis this does not mean that I pass through such a crisis. Though I may be affected as a citizen, I am, as an individual, the observer of something which does not happen to me.

whom pursues his own purposes (often competing against each other) or the purposes of the family or other associations —the state is a sphere having its own particular purposes. In this sphere they act as a single subject. In the consciousness of belonging together they realize the purpose which the national context prescribes for them. Indeed, in this whole, the consciousness of an—at the time—highest good for it, is formed. This occurs under the influence of a common mood or under the leadership of a great man, as in the time of Luther or Bismarck. Then the feeling of belonging together is present in the common purposes. Then, too, the outer events, destinies and actions are measured by the purpose which, at the time, represents the inner content of the nation's life. As no nation counts on its death, plans and purposes have quite a different place in its life from the one they have in the life of the individual. They always have only a temporal, relative, relation to the inwardness of the nation. For the latter is capable of infinite potentialities.

Thus, every form a nation takes is transitory. The possibility that one formative tendency should be supplemented by its contrary because of consciousness of its inadequacy is always at hand.

Thus, here, the concept of development is given a much more comprehensive but also more indeterminate meaning. The regular patterns which anthropology associates with passion, illusion, reason, idea or self-control vanish completely here. Every generation forgets the experiences of the one before.

Philosophers raise the problem—is the goal of every individual not within himself and does not the value of life lie only in an individual existence? In the positing of this question lies a transgression of all experience, a transition into an empty metaphysics of history; for my rejection of the philosophy of history means just this; that neither the above assumption (that values only acquire reality in individuals) nor the opposing view, that nations or mankind have an ascertainable goal of development, is in any way scientific. The common experiences of a nation, common purposes and memories are real. They are the source of the communally determined purposes of individuals. It is a commonplace that only individuals can experience the satisfaction of realized goals, the consciousness of common experience and of being sustained and filled by common memories. But, it does not follow from this that what takes place only in individuals exists only for their satisfaction. On the contrary, the fact is that an individual wills national purposes as his own, experiences national experiences and knows the memories of such experiences as his own and is filled and sustained by them. It is not possible to penetrate behind this reality which consists of the consciousness of value, meaning, purpose and good, by means of problematical, psychological, reasoning. We do not know directly as a fact how it happens that, as well as realizing a meaning related to the course of our own lives, we also find a meaning in life through these shared experiences. It is one of the many transgressions of explanatory psychology that it should occupy itself with aimless conjectures about this. These are on a par with the conjectures of those who, instead of describing religious experience as history reveals it, based it on their own feeble personal religious experience, tracing it back to selfishness and personal satisfaction.

But, equally pernicious transgressions occur when positive hypotheses are framed about the relation of personal consciousness to a real super-individual unit, whether this unit is determined transcendentally or in terms of racial psychology. These hypotheses are as inadmissible as those which maintain the reality of divine activity in the individual consciousness. The inference that there is a super-empirical subject manifesting itself in the individual consciousness is based on the consciousness of belonging together and the general validity of thinking and obligation, and marks the turning point from Kantian speculation to the transcendental method of construction. This assumes that a system of reality which will make these relations comprehensible underlies the facts of connection, of belonging together, of the exchangeability in the place of concepts and of binding obligation. The creation of this transcendental method is the death of history because it excludes the digging down into the realities just mentioned by means of fruitful historical concepts. Equally to be rejected is the transgression which bases historical connections on actual persons instead of making them the logical subjects of assertions which are different from those of individual psychology. Herbart,[1] who first conceived the idea of seeking out regular relations in communities, distinguishable from those in the individual soul, was far from making such an assumption.

Pages 185-187. Part II. Ages and Periods
In the course of historical events periods can be delimited in which a unity of mental climate embracing everything from the conditions of life up to the highest ideas, took shape, reached its zenith, and disintegrated again. In each such period there exists an inner structure, common to them all, which determines the connections of the parts to the whole, the course of events and the modifications in the tendencies; we shall see later what the comparative method can achieve for the comprehension of such structures. In the constant dynamism of the general structural relations we saw the meaning and significance of history. The way these are always active at every point and time and determine human life constitutes, primarily, the meaning of the mind-affected world. Our task is to study systematically from the bottom up, the regularities which make up the structure of the system of interactions within the individual and in the other units which are involved in them. We can only determine how far these structural laws make it possible to predict the future when this foundation has been laid. The unchanging, the regular, in historical processes is the first subject matter of study and, on it, the answer to all questions about progress in history and the direction in which humanity is moving, is dependent. The structure of a certain age was proved to be a system of subsystems and movements, in the great dynamic complex of that age. From highly varied and variable elements a complex whole forms. And this determines the meaning of all that is active in the age. If the spirit of such an age is born of grief and discord then every individual has his meaning through it

[1] Johann Friedrich Herbart, 1776-1841. Distinguished German philosopher, psychologist and educationalist.

and in it. The great historical persons are, above all, determined by this context. Their creative activity does not reach into historical distance but draws its goals from the values and meaning-context of the age itself. The productive energy of a nation at a certain time receives its greatest power from the fact that the human beings of the age are confined by its horizon; their labour serves the realization of the fundamental goals of the age. Thus they become its representatives.

Everything in an age derives its meaning from the energy which gives it its fundamental tendency. This expresses itself in stone and on canvas, in deeds or words. It objectifies itself in the constitution and legislation of the nations. Filled by it the historian comprehends former ages and, from its point of view, the philosopher tries to interpret the meaning of the world. All the expressions of the energy which determines the age are akin to each other. The task of analysis is to find the unity of valuation and purpose in different expressions of life. And, as the expressions tend towards absolute valuations and goals, the circle in which human beings of that age are enclosed completes itself; for, in it, the opposite tendencies are contained as well. We saw how the age imprints its stamp on them as well and how the dominant tendencies inhibit their free development. Thus the whole system of interactions of the age is determined from within by the links between life, the world of feelings, valuations and goals. Every activity which becomes part of this context is historical; the context forms the horizon of the age and, through it, finally, the meaning of every part in the system of the age is determined. This is the centring of ages and epochs on themselves in which the problem of the meaning and significance of history is solved.

Every age refers back to the preceding one, for the forces developed in the latter continue to be active in it; at the same time it already contains the strivings and creative activities which prepare for the succeeding age. As it arose from the insufficiency of the preceding one so it bears in itself the limits, tension, sufferings which prepare for the next age. As every shape which historical life takes is finite there must be a balance of joyful power and pressure, of expansion and narrowness of existence, of satisfaction and want. Its fundamental tendency reaches the height of effectiveness for a short time only. And, from one age to another the insatiable hunger for all kinds of satisfactions continues.

Whatever conclusions we may reach about the progressive composition of the structure of historical life in the relationship of historical ages and periods, impoverishment of existence, servitude and unfulfilled longing is involved in the ephemeral nature of every historical configuration. And this is primarily because power relations can never be eliminated from the living together of psycho-physical beings. Just as the autocracy of the age of Enlightenment produced 'cabinet wars' and exploitation of the subject for the sake of a life of luxury at court, as well as striving for the rational development of power, so every other arrangement of power relations has a double-edged effect. And the significance of history can only be sought in the meaning of all the forces which were linked together by the connections between different ages.

Pages 287-288. Part III. The Context of Universal History
Ages are structurally different from each other. In the Middle Ages interrelated ideas prevailed in the different spheres; the idea of loyalty in feudalism, the imitation of Christ in obedience, (the content of which is the transcendence of mind over nature through abnegation); the teleological hierarchy in the sciences. But it must be recognized that power is the background of these ideas and cannot be subjugated by this higher world.

And everywhere this is so; the facts of race, of place, of relations of forces, form a foundation which cannot be spiritualized. (It is a dream of Hegel's that the ages present stages in the development of reason.) To describe an age always presupposes a clear eye for these facts.

But there are inner connections which form the transition from the conditioning circumstances, the facts, the clash of forces, to the developments of ideals, etc.

Every given state of affairs in the infinite series precipitates a change because the *needs which release the existing energies into activity* can never be satisfied and the hunger for all kinds of satisfactions can never be satiated.

Every configuration of historical life is finite and, therefore, contains balanced against each other joyful power and pressure, expansion and narrowness of existence, satisfaction and deprivation, giving rise to power tensions and redistribution; thus actions constantly arise.

To summarize; only at a few points of historical life is there momentary calm. Its causes are different; balance of conflicting forces. History is movement.

But there is happiness, too, in progression. Tensions are dissolved; an ideal is realized, and so on.

Between dead, compelling fact and the highest spiritual life lies the constant development of organizations, of institutions, of regulated exercise of power. The intellect creates what we might call mechanisms for the satisfaction of needs and is constantly perfecting them. The purpose which the intellect posits produces these mechanisms. Railways are as much mechanisms of this kind as armies, factories and improvements of constitutions. They are the proper sphere of the intellect which seeks means for ends and calculates the consequences of actions.

Here a combination which discloses the essential nature of history is revealed. It is based on irrational factuality from which originates, on the one hand the distribution of tension (which also involves the mechanisms) and, on the other, the differentiation into individuals according to nationality, customs and thought. On this the real history of the mind-affected world rests.

CHAPTER VI

MEANING AND HISTORICAL
RELATIVITY

For this final chapter I have selected passages in which Dilthey restates eloquently his whole conception of history and takes issue with the problem of historical relativity. The subject matter of history is the life of mankind in time. The historical world is made up of individual human beings, their actions and productions. These individuals have intrinsic value and experience things as valuable; they have purposes and perceive their lives as meaningful. Because of this the historical world is teleological, permeated with values and meaningful. It is meaningful and, therefore, intelligible not because specific historical laws of change, development or progress can be detected in it, but because, throughout, the general laws of human nature apply and provide some principles of order and predictability. Nor does this present an absolute, unhistorical starting point. The epistemological circle which we have encountered before in the human studies applies here, too, for we know human nature from its historical manifestations.

Though concerned with the thoughts, feelings and purposes of human beings the historian need not rely on the uncertain tracing of hidden motives. These are often inaccessible to objective scrutiny and reliance on them would lead to historical scepticism. The historian can understand how human beings judged circumstances and interpreted their meaning and can appreciate—with a detachment gained from historical distance—what they valued because they have expressed themselves in scientific works, philosophic systems, literary productions and in the creation or maintenance of institutions. In their actions, too, their purposes are transparently clear. Finally, as the historian observes the unfolding of the consequences of an action beyond those intended by the actor, the action acquires new meaning for him. (His interpretation of the meaning of an action, though it may contain truth, cannot, therefore, at any point of time, be final and complete.)

It was Dilthey's general philosophic conviction that we cannot go behind life but can only try to understand it from within. Consistently with this view he rejected the application of any metaphysical scaffolding to history. History, too, must be understood from within. All meaning, all value, all purpose, in the historical world, is rooted in the experience of individual human beings who lived at a particular time and in particular circumstances. This raises the spectre of the historical relativity of all values and beliefs. The historian notes, as a fact, that, in all ages, human beings have held some values to be absolute and considered some religious or philosophic beliefs to be unconditionally true; but he is not concerned with the validity of these claims. He is aware of the variety of standards for which absolute validity has been claimed in different ages and places, observes the irreconcilable conflict between unconditionally held beliefs even within one age and nation and has no historical means of deciding between them. Even if he believes himself to be in possession of some absolute standard by means of which he could decide between all these conflicting claims, this would not help him as a historian. His task is to show how points of view, whether unconditionally valid or not, arose in particular historical circumstances and influenced the actions of those who accepted them. Does this mean that history must lead to timid indifference on moral issues and paralyse the springs of confident action? Dilthey's answer is as follows. Moral obligation does not, and need not, arise in a historical void. We feel the force of an obligation and are directed towards one course of action because we stand in a definite historically determined situation and because we are, as the result of historical processes, certain kinds of persons with certain feelings, ideas and convictions. But this does not mean determinism. The very consciousness of the historical relativity of all values represents the ultimate liberation of the human mind from all dogmatic narrowness. Awareness of different points of view widens our vision and the very fact that every position taken up by man is conditioned by time and place enables us to face new situations with free and creative action. In fact, historical relativity is merely the corollary of human freedom and creativeness.

TEXT

Pages 172 middle—173. Part II. The Mind-affected World as a System of Interactions
From analysing the historical world into individual systems of interactions there follows a conclusion which directs us towards the solution of the problem contained in the historical world. Comprehension of the meaning and significance of the historical world is often derived, as by Hegel or Comte, from ascertaining a general direction in the movement of universal history. This telescopes the interaction of many elements into one indeterminate vision. In fact we find that the historical movement takes place in the individual contexts of interactions. It further emerges that the whole search for the goal of history is completely one-sided. *The manifest meaning of history must, first of all, be sought in what is always present*, in what always recurs in the structural relations, in the patterns of interactions, in the formation of values and purposes in them, in the inner order in which they are related to each other, that is, in everything from the structure of the individual life up to the last all-embracing unit; this is the meaning which history always has; it rests on the structure of the individual existence and reveals itself through the objectifications of life, in the composite patterns of interactions. This regularity determines the past development and the future is subject to it. The analysis of the construction of the mind-affected world will, above all, have to show these regularities in the structure of the historical world.

*Pages 255-256. Part III. The Historical World and Meaning.
Value and History*

The historical categories of value and purpose grow out of
lived experience. But when the experiencing subject looks
backward meaning already makes its appearance in his understanding and this implies connectedness as a category.

Whenever connections occur in history and wherever there
is freedom within reality we must apply the concept of
meaning. Wherever life is past and has entered understanding
there is history. And where history is there is meaning in all
its variety. Where an individual represents something more
comprehensive, gathers it up, and, as it were, makes it totally
visible in himself, meaning is present. It is present wherever
a particular change of the whole pattern occurs through an
event, an individual or a community. (In history there is never
the idea of a mere sum of consequences.)

In the historical world, too, the relation between values and
the constant flaming up and dying away of personal feelings
persist. Here, too, no value which is not connected with it has
reality. A confusing, infinite manifold, an infinite horizon
opens up here. It is as if at nightfall we were looking down
on to a strange city, the lights of which go up, become
stronger, vanish and are lost in a no longer visible distance.
But all this light and sparkle belongs to an objective world
which is strange and remote in space and time. Thus the
historical meaning of the concepts of contemplation and value
is developed further. The life of particular individuals is complete. Their intrinsic value can be surveyed as a whole. A new
assessment of values which no longer has anything to do with
practical conduct, emerges. The line of gradations upwards
from the average man gives us the norm of the highest intrinsic values which we know; the farther back the eye
penetrates into the past the more remote and objective do
these values become, for the effect of historical remoteness is
the same as the effect of remoteness given by people por-
trayed in a work of art. Even the possibility of comparing our
own destiny and value with something historical vanishes.

In this manifold of historical values there emerges the
difference between things which have only utilitarian value

and those which have intrinsic value and are conscious of themselves. These values are the material of the historical world. They are like notes from which the web of melodies of the mind-affected universe emerges. Each of them assumes a fixed position in this web according to the relations in which it stands to others. But each not only has the definiteness of a note, according to its loudness, pitch and length, but, as an individual he is something indefinable, unique, not only according to the relation in which he stands but also of himself.

Life is the fullness, variety and interaction—within something continuous—experienced by individuals. Its subject matter is identical with history. At every point of history there is life. And history consists of life of every kind in the most varied circumstances. History is merely life viewed in terms of the continuity of mankind as a whole.

Those individuals with their purposes and meaning, who, as intrinsic values, form life and history, are, above all, effective forces consciously animated by values, and relate themselves to the pragmatic value of things; they are, in fact, purposive. Thus the historical world is full of purposes, is seen purely as a manifold of forces—a purpose-filled world.

Page 341. Part IV. The States in the Age of Enlightenment
There is a relation, strange as it is important, between purpose and meaning, which we have already noticed in the life of the individual, and which asserts itself in history. States and rulers pursue their ends. In this they are limited by the horizon of their age. They act for themselves, not for the whole of mankind, or for history. But the meaning of what they do in the context of history becomes visible only to later ages; it extends far beyond the ends which they had set themselves. There is nothing mystical in this; we need not trouble providence or a purpose pursued by history itself. As time progresses the wider context reveals the consequences of purposive actions so that they appear as parts of a context which, later perhaps, may emerge into a wider context still. What we see is always only a limited relation between elements of history and the whole of the past. But what is decisive is that

we see a real, though limited, meaning; in no succeeding context can it be cancelled. Hence the historian sees truly.

Pages 259-261. Part III. Historical Scepticism
Meaning or value cannot be possessed by something which cannot be understood. A tree can never have a meaning . . .

The main argument of historical sceptics is always that the way actions are determined by motives is uncertain; for the individual has only uncertain knowledge of his own motives and others have still less insight. The contribution of selfishness, ambition, lust for power, or vanity, to decisive actions can not be adequately ascertained. Even oral expressions or statements in letters remain questionable. But this is the proper field of what experts on human nature and men of the world take to be true history . . .

Historical scepticism can only be overcome if historical method does not have to count on ascertaining motives and if the understanding of structures created by the mind takes the place of psychological subtleties. They lie before us as something externally objectified and can become the subject matter of disciplined understanding.

They[1] fall into three classes. Understanding achieves the highest degree of certainty in the interpretation of the scientific mind.

A lesser degree is found in the products of practical wisdom, religion, art and philosophy. These are partly expressions of the context of our own lives and partly representations of the whole context of life.

The third and most difficult class is formed by the sphere of actions and the setting of purposes. The relation between the setting of purposes, the finding of means and action is rational and transparent; but the motives which determine the setting of purposes are a different matter. Actions of general import which become historical are not accompanied by consciousness of motive. But they have clear connections with the objective necessities which are embodied in the purposive systems and outer organizations; at the same time their motives are quite irrelevant to their effects; these depend only

[1] i.e. structures created by the mind.

on the ideas of purpose and possible means. Thus the systematic human studies concerned with the world of action are the foundation for a sure understanding of that world.

Here the inclusion of comparisons, etc., complicates the method of understanding.

Page 173. Part II. The Mind-affected World as a System of Interactions

This also disposes of the view that the task of history is to proceed from relative to absolute values, obligations, norms and goods. If we did this we would step from the sphere of empirical studies into that of speculation. History does indeed know of the positing of something unconditional as value, norm or good. These occur everywhere in it—sometimes as given in the divine will, sometimes in a rational concept of perfection, in a teleological system of the world, in a universally valid, transcendentally based, norm of our actions. But historical experience knows only the processes of positing, which are important to it and nothing of their universal validity. By tracing the course of development of such unconditional values, goods or norms, it notices that life has produced different ones and that the unconditional positing itself only becomes possible because the horizon of the age is limited. Then it looks at the totality of life in the fullness of its historical manifestations. It notices the unsettled conflict among these unconditional positings. The question whether the subordination to something unconditional, which, after all, is a historical fact, can be traced back with logical conclusiveness to a universal, not temporally limited, condition in man, or must be viewed as a product of history, leads ultimately to the profundities of transcendental philosophy which lie beyond the empirical sphere of history and from which even the philosopher cannot extract a certain answer. And, even if this question were definitely settled it would not help the historian in his selecting, understanding and tracing of connections if the content of what is taken as unconditional could not be determined. Thus the intervention of speculation into the empirical sphere of the historian can scarcely reckon on success. The historian cannot renounce the attempt to understand history from within on the basis of an analysis of the different contexts of interactions.

Page 289-291. Part III. Reality, Value, Culture. The Problem of Value in History. Conclusion of the Treatise

If we eliminate the foundation in transcendental philosophy then there is no method for ascertaining unconditional norms, values or purposes. There are only those which claim unconditional validity but which, because of their origin, are tainted with relativity.

But, we do, in fact, measure meaning in terms of some real or ideal context in relation to which a person or an event acquires this characteristic . . .

One aspect at least is clear; what I find significant in the present is what is fruitful for the future, for my actions in it and for the progress of society towards it.

And here I see clearly, from a practical point of view that I must start from universally valid judgements about the object of my endeavour if I am to control the future. The present does not contain circumstances but processes and systems of interactions. These reach towards a future attainment which can be achieved. Bismarck's statement that he had been placed by his religion and his state into a position in which service to that state was more important than all cultural tasks was generally valid for him because it was based on religion. From this it follows that, in retrospect, we have to assume the same relationship. In an age general norms, values and purposes arise and the meaning of an action has to be grasped in relation to them. According to whether these are only conditionally, or unconditionally, determined there is a further difference. It appears that even within one nation there is conflict about values.

So we arrive, on a deeper level, at the statement that the development of such ideas moves in contradictions (Kant, Hegel) contained in the course of the formation of institutions, etc. These are then formulated and, again and again, their relation to each other makes a wider and freer position possible. There are, to start with, no values which are valid for all nations. In the Roman empire there developed an aristocratic conception of mankind as the bearer of humanitas. In Christianity the notion of mankind as something of value arose and this notion was given fresh emphasis in the Age of Enlightenment. History itself is the productive force for the creation of valuations, ideals and purposes by which the significance of people and events is measured . . .

It is said that the consciousness of relativity thus arises in history. No doubt every historical phenomenon is finite and, therefore relative . . .

The final problem of a critique of historical reason along the lines indicated in this; in history there is already formation and selection in the search for the inner connections. There is always progression in accordance with the conditions of finitude, suffering, power, contrast and accumulation which connects one part of history with another; and power, values meaning and purpose are the links in which the connections of history lie. But are the experienced connections, the experienced values, meaning and purpose the last word of the historian?

My line of argument is determined by the following statements

1. The concept of value arises from life.
2. The norm for every judgement, etc., is given in the relative conceptions of meaning, value and purpose of nations and ages.
3. The task is to describe how these have widened out into something absolute.
4. To sum up, this means the total recognition of the immanence to historical consciousness of even the unconditionally held values and norms.

The historical consciousness of the finitude of every historical phenomenon, of every human or social condition and of the relativity of every kind of faith, is the last step towards the liberation of man. With it man achieves the sovereignty to enjoy every experience to the full and surrender himself to it unencumbered, as if there were no system of philosophy or faith to tie him down. Life is freed from knowledge through concepts; the mind becomes sovereign over the cobwebs of dogmatic thought. Everything beautiful, everything holy, every sacrifice relived and interpreted, opens perspectives which disclose some part of reality. And equally, we accept the evil, horrible and ugly, as filling a place in the world, as containing some reality which must be justified in the system of things, something which cannot be conjured away. And, in contrast to relativity, the continuity of creative forces asserts itself as the central historical fact.

Thus a view of life arises from experience, understanding, poetry and history and forms a constant background. Reflection only raises it to analytical precision and clarity. The teleological view of the world and of life is recognized as a metaphysical system resting on a one-sided, not fortuitous but partial, vision of life. The doctrine of the objective value of life as a metaphysical system transcends what can be known. But we experience connections between life and history in which each part has significance. [The parts of] life and history have meaning as letters have in a word. Just as there are particles and conjugations so there are syntactical elements in life and man seeks their significance in various ways. The attempt used to be made to grasp life through the world. But there is only the one road from the interpretation of life to the world and life is only there in experience, understanding and historical apprehension. We do not carry the meaning of the world into life. We are open to the possibility that meaning and significance arise only in man and his history, not in the isolated individual but in man as a historical being. For man is something historical.

INDEX

Key references only are given for terms which occur frequently. The figures in italics refer to Dilthey's text.

GEORGE ALLEN & UNWIN LTD
London: 40 Museum Street, W.C.1

Auckland: 24 Wyndham Street
Bombay: 15 Graham Road, Ballard Estate, Bombay 1
Buenos Aires: Escritorio 454-459, Florida 165
Calcutta: 17 Chittaranjan Avenue, Calcutta 13
Cape Town: 109 Long Street
Hong Kong: F1/12 Mirador Mansions, Kowloon
Karachi: Karachi Chambers, McLeod Road
Madras: Mohan Mansion, 38c Mount Road, Madras 6.
Mexico: Villalongin 32-10, Piso, Mexico 5, D.F.
New Delhi: 13-14 Ajmeri Gate Extension, New Delhi 1
Sao Paulo: Avenida 9 de Julho 1138-Ap. 51
Singapore: 36c Prinsep Street, Singapore 7
Sydney, N.S.W.: Bradbury House, 55 York Street
Toronto: 91 Wellington Street West

THE TIDES OF HISTORY
Volume 1. *From the Beginnings to Islam*

JAQUES PIRENNE

'History', the author writes in his Preface, 'is essentially a continuity and a unity; a continuity that goes on, without men being able to escape it, from generation to generation, and which links our own times to the most distant epochs; a unity, since in any society the life of each man is bound up with the lives of all others, even as, in the community of nations, the history of each nation develops, without even being aware of it, as a part of the history of all the nations of the universe. . . .

'Confronted by the abyss into which humanity has fallen, should we not take stock and examine our consciences? There is no other way to do so, in my opinion, than to follow the long adventure of humanity. Only universal history, by comparing all civilizations, can cause some sort of philosophy of history to become apparent, and thus lead to sociological, scientific and moral conclusions. It alone is capable, by revealing to us that neither our country nor our race nor our age has achieved a civilization in all ways superior to all that has gone before, of eradicating those prejudices of religion, race and language, of political, social or mystical ideologies, that have not ceased to drive men into vain massacres and to degrade, by hatred, all ideals, even the noblest and those which have no other aim than the triumph of tolerance and love. Universal history also is alone able, by developing before our eyes the great cycles of human evolution, to make us understand at what point in evolution we are today. That, I think, is the essential question. For it is on knowledge of the necessities and possibilities of our time that the value of future peace depends.'

Jacques Pirenne, the distinguished Belgian historian, and son of the equally distinguished Henri Pirenne, has now completed a study of universal history in seven volumes, covering the whole of civilization from the beginnings to the most recent events of the 1950's. The first volume to be published in English, which ends with the advent of Islam, includes all the civilizations of antiquity from the earliest movements on the deltas of the Nile, the Indus, the Euphrates and Tigris, through the histories of Ancient Egypt, Babylon, Assyria, Persia, Greece, Rome and China and other parts of Asia. Gigantic in its scope, this study is remarkable for its lucidity, its comprehensiveness and its great readability.

Demy 8vo. Illustrated with 33 maps. About 50s net

HISTORY OF MANKIND
CULTURAL AND SCIENTIFIC DEVELOPMENT
(*To be complete in 7 volumes*)

Volume 1. *Prehistory and the Beginnings of Civilization*

JACQUETTA HAWKES and SIR LEONARD WOOLLEY

Part One—Early Peoples and Cultures: This volume is concerned with man's prehistoric past. Starting with the early ape-men and their first groping efforts to make tools, control fire and to form a language, it passes on to the emergence of *Homo-sapiens*, the differentiation of races and the peopling of the Americas. The material culture, religion and magnificent artistic creations of these latest Old Stone Age hunters are fully considered and illustrated. The story is taken down to the domestication of plants and animals in South-west Asia and the earliest spread of farming in Europe and Asia. There is also an account of the origins of agriculture in the New World. Men could now live a settled life and develop fine crafts; the way to civilization lay open before them. While presenting the facts of archaeology, the author has throughout attempted to give some insight into human experience during the hundreds of thousands of years of our prehistory.

Part Two—From the Introduction of Metal to 1200, B.C.: The Bronze Age saw the birth of civilization as contrasted with the conditions of the Neolithic period. By the end of that period, great parts of Europe, Asia and Africa were sparsely peopled by farmers living in small but largely self-sufficient settlements. Out of this virtually static condition was evolved the modern world. This volume describes easily and vividly the revolution in man's way of life and thought which began first in Mesopotamia and in the valleys of the Nile, the reasons for it and the way in which it came about.

It continues with grouping and distribution of mankind throughout the Bronze Age, the gradual urbanization of civilizations, the social and economic structures, the evolution of industries in pottery, glass, ivory and textiles and the development of science, fine arts, music and literature. Other chapters deal with religion, education, communication and travel. The book concludes with descriptions of the conditions of civilized life at the end of the thirteenth century, B.C.

Small Royal 8vo. Illustrated. About 42s net

PAUL MURRAY KENDALL

THE YORKIST AGE

The Yorkist Age unfolds the panorama of daily life during the Wars of the Roses. This first full-length study of English society in the fifteenth century draws upon contemporary narratives of travellers, the Paston Letters and other less widely known collections of correspondence, observations of French and Italian diplomats, town records, ecclesiastical reports, the literature of the age, chronicles, household and estate accounts, wills, chancery proceedings, and other revealing sources, in order to recreate the substance and the flavour of the life of the time.

Ideas, attitude, fears, aspirations, the 'olde daunce' of love and death, as well as the dress of the age, housekeeping in town and country, recreation and the state of business and the way of court-ship are caught in action, as they display themselves in the histories, proud and humble, of hundreds of people.

The Yorkist Age deals with pirates and members of Parliament, with merchants, minstrels, lords and lawyers, with ladies in love, ambitious yeomen and bored nuns.

Contrary to Shakespeare and popular belief, the Wars of the Roses had comparatively little effect upon the lives of the people as a whole and represented rather a recovery from than a descent into anarchy. The story of modern England opens not with the Tudors but in this Yorkist realm, a fascinating period of beginnings-and-endings, prosperously balanced between the upheavals of the late fourteenth century and the hard times and hard feelings of the early sixteenth.

'It may even be that we shall find in the reign of Edward IV the Age that subsequent centuries looked back to as Merrie England.'

Demy 8vo. Illustrated. About 35s net

RICHARD THE THIRD

2nd Impression. Sm. Roy. 8vo. Illustrated. 30s. net

WARWICK THE KINGMAKER

Sm. Roy. 8vo. Illustrated. 30s. net

INTERPRETATIONS OF HISTORY

ALBAN G. WIDGERY

One of the most broadly erudite scholars of our time—contemporaneous with Dr. Arnold Toynbee—the author has made a life-long study of the *meanings* given to history. In this volume, he presents an exposition of those meanings. Part I describes the conceptions of history implied in wide-spread religions and cultures, Confucian and Taoist, Hindu and Buddhist, Zoroastrian and Muslim, Greek and Roman, Jewish and Christian. Part II surveys the theories of independent thinkers and schools in the Occident from the Middle Ages to our own day. Eight scholars have reviewed the chapters dealing with their fields of study. Intending the book for general readers as well as for historians and philosophers, the author has eliminated all unnecessary diversions, such as footnotes. The writing is in that clear direct simple style that has distinguished his previous volumes. We know of no other book that deals with its subject. *Demy 8vo. About 28s net*

DAILY LIFE IN RUSSIA
Under the Last Tsar

HENRI TROYAT

For this study of life in Russia before the Revolution, the author has drawn not only upon the numerous records and reminiscences made available by others, but also upon his own childhood memories of Tsarist Russia and the tales of his parents. But to avoid treating the past as if it were dead matter, he has animated it by giving it the colour and vitality of a contemporary report. He has invented a traveller, new to the scene, who discovers Tsarist Russia for himself in all its many aspects: family life, religious activity, the conditions of the workers and peasants, housing, the machinery of government and the law, life in the army, entertainments, food and drink, festivals, the life of the royal family and its familiars as well as that of the outlaws of society and the deportees, and many other aspects great and small of everyday life at the beginning of the century. *Demy 8vo. Illustrated. About 28s net*

GREEK CIVILIZATION

Volume 1. *From the Iliad to the Parthenon*

Small Crown 4to.   Illustrated.   30s. net

Volume 2. *From the Antigone to Socrates*

Small Crown 4to.   Illustrated.   30s. net

Volume 3. *From Euripides to Alexandria*

ANDRÉ BONNARD

André Bonnard, the great Swiss Hellenist, lived just long enough to complete this, the third and concluding volume of his comprehensive study of Greek civilization. It is in every way a worthy successor to the volume that was described as 'the best popular introduction to Greek civilization that I have ever read' (Professor J. A. K. Thomson), and 'a fresh book, beautiful and truthful' (Stevie Smith).

This last volume covers the age of decline, the two centuries (the 4th and 3rd B.C.) that witnessed the death of the city states which were the social framework of the classical age. Demosthenes, their champion, was foredoomed to defeat, and the genius of Alexander, and of his father Philip, dealt them a mortal blow, though at the same time it was Alexander who created the shape of the modern state. During these two centuries there were philosophers like Plato and Aristotle, still trying to restore the old city state; but it was Plato who substituted for the earthly city a divine world where all would be gathered after death, thus pre-figuring the Heavenly City. In this way Greek civilization, as it declined, prepared the way for Christianity.

The first chapters are dedicated, however, to Euripides, a poet of the classical age who nevertheless foreshadows the decline. The chapters that follow include the study of Thucydides, Demosthenes, Plato, Aristotle, Alexander, the first two Ptolemys, Alexandrian astronomy (Aristarchus), geography (Pytheas and Eratosthenes, medical science, Archimedes, and the poetry of Callimachus, Apollonius and Theocritus. The book ends with a chapter on Epicurus.

Thus the scope of this volume is much wider than that of its predecessors, but the handling of the material is no less masterly. It is profusely and beautifully illustrated.

Small Crown 4to.   Illustrated.   About 35s net

GEORGE ALLEN & UNWIN LTD